# MY TEENAGE DREAM ENDED

A MEMOIR

## FARRAH ABRAHAM

**MTV PRESS**

New York

FIRST PUBLISHED IN THE UNITED STATES OF AMERICA IN 2012 BY:
MTV Press
1515 Broadway
New York, NY 10036
mtv.com

This work is a memoir. It reflects the author's present recollection of her experiences over a period of years. Certain names, locations, and identifying characteristics have been changed. Dialogue and events have been recreated from memory, and, in some cases, have been compressed to convey the substance of what was said or what occurred.

The views and opinions expressed in the book are solely those of the author and do not represent the views of MTV or its parent company, Viacom, Inc.

Designed by Susan H. Choi

Photography on pages 162 and 176 by Justin Riddle,
Total Event Photography,
ph: 402.813.2156 email: Justinriddle1@gmail.com

DISTRIBUTED BY
powerHouse Books
37 Main Street, Brooklyn, NY 11201
PHONE 212 604 9074 FAX 212 366 5247
powerHouseBooks.com

FIRST EDITION
2012 / 10 9 8 7 6 5 4 3 2 1

PRINTED AND BOUND IN THE UNITED STATES OF AMERICA

ISBN: 978-1576875988

*In loving memory of Derek*

*My first love, from whom I learned so much.*

*Rest in peace.*

*To my daughter, Sophia*

*Thank you for bringing meaning, happiness,*

*and unconditional motherly love into my life.*

*To my parents*

*Thank you for helping me get through these tough years.*

# CONTENTS

# CONTENTS

# CONTENTS

# PROLOGUE

My teenage dream ended when I was seventeen. All it took was a phone call. One phone call, and my dream was gone forever.

Up until that moment, I had it all. I was confident, popular, a cheerleader. Best of all, I was crazy in love: The Real Thing. We were lovers and best friends. When we were together, the rest of the world melted away. Sure we had plenty of drama. We made love, fought and broke up, then made up and made love again.

Even when I accidentally got pregnant, I was convinced that everything would work out in the end. We were meant to be together. We wanted to get married and have children. It was just happening sooner than we had planned.

Then, a friend's voice on the phone changed everything.

"Derek died in a car wreck last night."

Just like that, my teenage dream ended.

# THE PHONE CALL
# THAT CHANGED MY LIFE

I woke up from an uncomfortable sleep to the sound of my cell phone ring-ing.  It was December 28$^{th}$ and I had fallen asleep downstairs in my parent's bedroom while watching a movie with my mom.  I didn't usually sleep in my parent's bed, but my mother had wanted me to sleep with her that night. She was worried about me because lately I had turned from a confident social butterfly into a quiet, sad and lonely girl.

I was torn between letting it go and picking it up.  I couldn't tell if my mom was asleep and I didn't want her listening in on my call, but I knew there must be some drama going on for anyone to be calling me in the middle of the night these days.  I had distanced myself from my usual crowd of friends, trying not to get caught up in immature gossip or going out late at night. I was seventeen and seven months pregnant.  I was going to be on TV soon. I wanted to change my life and get on a better path, for both my baby and myself.

The ringing stopped and I saw the missed call was from Kerrie, one of the few people I could still call a true friend.  The last couple of times we had talked it was about boyfriend problems, but it had been a while.  There was no message, so I figured she was calling to tell me that she'd seen Derek, my ex, flirting with some girl at a party. He and I played that game; flirting in public, knowing word would get back, just to make the other jealous.

It was 3 AM and I was too tired to hear about his latest flirtation, so I went back to sleep. But the next morning when I woke up, curiosity got the better of me and I had to know why Kerrie had been calling in the middle of the night. I missed Derek and wanted to talk about him, even if it was just to hear that he was hooking up with some girl to make me jealous.

We were already "officially" broken up when I found out I was pregnant. He had tried to call me when word got out about my pregnancy, but I was determined to keep my distance until after the baby was born. I needed a break from the drama and time to figure out what it meant now that we had a baby on the way. The distance was meant to show him how serious I was and how serious I needed him to be.

My mom was already upstairs cooking breakfast in the kitchen, so I hauled my big belly out of bed and called Kerrie back. She picked up on the first ring. She didn't say hello. She just said, "Derek died in a car wreck last night." I don't remember much else about the conversation—what I said, what she said. I only remember that one sentence. I can still hear her saying it, even now, years later.

*Derek died in a car wreck last night.*

I got off the phone and tried to calm down, but my mind was racing. Derek was the father of the baby I was carrying inside me. He was my first love, my only true love. We hadn't spoken in more than two months, but I had still believed we had a future together—me, him, and our baby, as one happy family. It's every teenage girl's dream, right? You meet a boy, you fall in love, and then one day you have a family and grow old together, happily ever after. 'Til death do us part.

Now Derek was gone forever, and so was my happy ending.

At breakfast I sat quietly, trying not to choke on my cereal. It must have been obvious that something was wrong, because my mom brought up my phone ringing in the middle of the night. She asked if it was one of Derek's friends trying to get hold of me. She knew that his friends were sending me messages on the computer, which I kept ignoring.

"Is Derek trying to start more issues?" my mom asked. She didn't wait for me to answer and just launched into her usual string of derogatory comments about him. She hated Derek; she was furious that I was pregnant with his baby and wanted him to stay out of my life.

Usually, I just ignored what my mom had to say about Derek, but this morning, of all mornings, I couldn't take it. I yelled, "He's dead!" and ran upstairs to my room.

After that, my parents barely said another word about Derek. I know that they read the same news stories and watched the same TV reports that I did. Yet they acted like he had never existed. We had been caught sneaking around too many times and they thought he was a bad influence on me. I felt like they were relieved that he was out of the picture—forever. Their hatred of him seemed to make them blind to my grief. The few times I tried to talk to them, they dismissed the subject. My mom would say, "Some things happen for a reason. Maybe him not being here is better for you and your baby." Or my dad would chime in with, "Yeah, you never know, you could have been in the car with Derek and then you both would have been killed."

So I stopped talking to them about him.

I stopped talking to anyone about him. Words felt useless anyway. There was no way to describe the grief that had settled over my world. Nothing I could say would make the pain go away. So I locked my memories of Derek away and focused on getting my life on track for our baby—she was all I had left of Derek now.

# I MET HIM AT A BASKETBALL GAME

———••◦⟨∞⟩◦••———

Derek wasn't my first boyfriend, but he was my first love. I still remember almost every detail about the night we met. I was fifteen and had my first "real" boyfriend—though it wasn't serious. I was at that age when I was curious about the opposite sex and wanted to find out what guys were like.

I knew exactly the kind of guy I wanted: preppy, with a job and a car, who would take me out and be my best friend. I wanted what most teen girls dream of—that ideal boyfriend who would whisk me away into a world of love and happiness. When I met Derek, I thought he would be that guy.

The night I met him, a friend called to say she was going to a high school basketball game and wondered if I wanted to come. I had recently switched schools and hadn't seen her in a while. I was looking forward to catching up and arranged to meet her there. I told her I was trying to end it with my boyfriend, but that we still might come together. She said she had just started dating this new guy and wanted me to meet him.

When we arrived at the game, my boyfriend immediately ditched me to go sit with his guy friends—typical jock. This was one of the reasons I wanted to end it with him—I didn't feel like he really respected me or appreciated being with me. Instead of getting mad, though, I kept my cool and went to find my friend.

I found her hanging out with a bunch of friends from my old school. She introduced me, but I could tell none of them was the boyfriend she'd mentioned. "So, where's this new boyfriend?" I asked.

She laughed. "He should be on his way. I don't know why he's late."

This detail should have been a red flag. Guys who are late, guys who say they will show up somewhere and then don't, or come late—that's not a good sign. But I was too young and inexperienced to know any better.

I went back to watch the game and at halftime wandered over to see my friend again, and there he was. She said, "This is Farrah," and when I looked up at him she said, "and this is Derek."

I didn't say anything. I just smiled, but it felt like a jolt of electricity was running through my body. He was good looking—light brown hair, hazel eyes, tan—and wore light jeans with a beige cotton coat over a button-down shirt and a simple chain around his neck. A super preppy guy—just what I liked.

I was taken aback by my strong reaction to him. I liked him immediately, but he was dating my friend, so I kept my mouth shut. I have a strict policy about going after friends' boyfriends. But I was aware of him the whole game, sitting a row behind me with his buddies. I had never felt like that about a guy before.

Even though he wasn't available, just meeting Derek changed my life. For one thing, I totally got over my boyfriend and broke up with him.

# BEST ST. PATRICK'S DAY EVER!

Though I knew Derek was off-limits, I couldn't stop thinking about him.  We went to different high schools, so it was unlikely I would see him again if I didn't take matters into my own hands. Finally, I couldn't take it anymore and called my friend to find out how serious she was about Derek.  She had a short attention span when it came to guys, so it was possible they had already broken up. I tried to sound casual as we chatted, but all I really wanted to know about was Derek.  Finally I slipped in, "So what happened to that boy at the basketball game?"

She snorted. "You mean Derek? Oh, that was short-lived. I'm into someone else now." Derek was available! I got off the phone as fast as I could without seeming rude and immediately logged onto Myspace and found his page. I messaged him, but played it cool, saying something like, "Hey, nice meeting you at the basketball game. We should go out sometime. What are you doing for St. Patrick's Day?"

It took him two days to message me back, but when he did he said he was going to a St. Patrick's Day party and asked me to come with him. So I gave him my number.  I was so excited, I could barely stand it.  Of course, when

Derek and his friend came to pick me up, I still played it cool. I just said, "Hey" and acted like I was all about being chill and hanging with him *and* his friends.

We drove to a party way out somewhere in Omaha. On the way we saw cops everywhere, and the guys were freaking out about random police checkpoints because they had alcohol in the car.

We pulled up at the party house and there was music playing and lots of kids from my school were hanging out, playing Guitar Hero and drinking games, all happy that it was a holiday. It was a fun atmosphere and we joined the party. I was still playing it cool with Derek and his friends, just hanging out, like maybe I wasn't that interested—even though I totally was. I didn't flirt with him; I always maintain class in front of other people and I wasn't going to hang all over him like a groupie, no matter how into him I was. Plus, I wanted to see how he treated me and other people before I decided for sure if we should date.

Derek must have been on the same wavelength, because he didn't flirt with me much, either. We mostly chatted with other people at the party, but every once in a while our eyes would meet. It was like a fun, sexy game that made me want to date him even more.

At the end of the night we headed home in Derek's friend's car. Derek and I sat in the back together. My head was spinning, whether from the alcohol I drank or from being so close to Derek I wasn't sure. The next thing I knew, though, Derek and I were making out, right there in the backseat, for straight-up an hour. It didn't seem like an hour had gone by, but I checked my watch and time doesn't lie. That's what it was always like with Derek, an hour would feel like a minute.

Suddenly the car stopped and we were in front of my house. Derek kissed me one last time and said, "I'll call you tomorrow."

As I walked through my front door, I was floating on air. The night had gone even better than I could have imagined.

That was the best St. Patrick's Day ever!

# SEALED WITH A KISS

We went on a few dates after that—dinner, the movies, and a few more parties—and started spending all our free time together. We would go on long walks in the Old Market, ConAgra Park, or along the river, talking for hours. This felt way different from what I had experienced with my first boyfriend. Derek was thoughtful and romantic—he would text me all the time when we weren't together and surprise me with flowers. Sometimes he would just show up at my house late at night and throw pebbles at my window to wake me up and surprise me when he got off work. I was so into him and I could tell he really liked me, too.

A couple of weeks after that St. Patrick's Day party, on April 1st, Derek asked me to be his girlfriend. One night, after a long session of hanging out, playing Guitar Hero and beer pong, we had ended up crashing at his friend's sister's apartment. We were cuddling in bed and talking randomly when all of a sudden he asked, "Do you want to be my girlfriend?" I didn't even have to think about it. "Yes!" I answered immediately and snuggled into him. It wasn't ideal, he didn't get down on a bended knee or anything, but I was so happy that he wanted us to be "official" that it felt as romantic as a marriage proposal. That was the first night we fell asleep in each other's arms.

Whenever we hung out we would hold hands and hug, but I wouldn't kiss him if I wasn't tipsy. I always felt so nervous and shy around him. Eventually, he mentioned the awkwardness of us only kissing when we partied. Derek seemed as nervous around me as I was around him and I wanted to prove to him that I really liked him.

I tried talking to my sister about how nerve-wracking it is to kiss someone for the first time. I worried about it not happening perfectly. I would think about things like, *If I shut my eyes will I miss his lips and kiss his cheek? How long should we kiss? Should I pull away first, or wait for him to end the kiss?* Being tipsy took the stress off because if you made a mistake you could always blame the alcohol. My sister just laughed and made fun of me. She didn't understand how much I liked Derek and how perfect I wanted our first sober kiss to be.

The next time we went out to a party I deliberately didn't drink and I kissed him anyway. We were standing by the stairs in the middle of the party and I just went for it. I didn't care who saw. I had intended to go in for a short sweet kiss, which was what I thought I could handle. But Derek wasn't having it and pulled me in for a long, passionate one. It felt like our mouths were magnetized and I was helpless to resist. I was too scared to pull away so it went on for a while. Eventually, I heard our friends yelling, "ew" and "quit kissing." I didn't let it bother me, though. I was so proud that we were having our first real kiss I felt like saying, *You all wish!*

That was a crazy night, with a lot of romantic drama—some couples were breaking up, others were hooking up for the first time. It was also the night that almost everyone we knew realized that Derek and I were a couple. Our kiss left no doubt about that. Hopefully, it would keep away all the girls who were always hovering around Derek, like sharks circling their prey.

A friend took a party photo of us kissing that night and every time I look at that picture, I can still feel the thrill of that moment.

# SISTER SISTER

That night, I ended up staying at Derek's friend's place with him and in the morning we all went out for breakfast. I felt like I was really starting to get to know Derek and his friends, which was great, but I began to notice that he was always hanging out at his buddies' houses instead of his own. He never talked about his family. I didn't know what was going on.

It bothered me that I still didn't know anything about his parents or his family life. That felt weird to me. Other guys I had dated had been open about their families, but it wasn't the same with Derek. He never mentioned his parents.

Then one day Derek picked me up from school and said we had to go get one if his sisters from her high school. I was happy to go along, happy he was finally letting me meet someone in his family.

When his sister got into the car with her friend, everything went really quiet and awkward. I had thought this was going to be my chance to bond with one of his sisters, but no one spoke the entire ride. We stopped to get gas and as Derek got out of the car his sister pointed her head towards me and said something like, "She's actually pretty." Derek smiled and went to pump the gas. I just said, "Thank you." It was such a weird comment. What was I supposed to say?

We dropped his sister and her friend off at Derek's house, and as we were leaving, his other sister pulled up in her car. They had a conversation about where their mom was, and while they were talking she was looking over at me, obviously checking me out. She never said one word to me, not even "hi" or "bye," but from the way she was looking at me, I could tell she was going to say something about me to Derek later.

I thought it was pretty rude of her not to talk to me, but I stayed neutral and didn't say anything to Derek. I didn't understand what was going on, but I didn't want to make trouble for him.

# FALLING IN

The next week Derek wanted to hang out with me a lot. I suggested we go fishing.  I knew my dad had fishing rods, so I thought it would be a good opportunity for him to meet my dad.  My parents were separated at the time, so Derek and I drove out to my dad's house to get the rods and the two of them met for the first time. It went great; my dad seemed to like Derek.  When he came down to meet us at Derek's car they shook hands and my dad said, "Here you go. I hope you guys have fun." I was happy that my dad accepted Derek. I always wanted my parents' approval and I (usually) tried hard not to disappoint them.

We went to my friend Sarah's house and fished in the lake in her back-yard. Derek and I sat at the end of the dock, chatting while we waited for the fish to bite.  It was so cute and perfect and he was such an outdoorsy, manly guy—I loved it!

After a while he said, "We're not going to catch any fish here. We should detach this dock and go out further."

I have always been scared of going out further into the lake and jumping on and off moving docks. I'm always afraid of falling in. But I didn't want Derek to see how chicken I was, so I said okay.

Sarah came outside and I told her that Derek wanted to detach the dock and go out farther. To Derek she said, "My brothers do it all the time—it should be fine." Then she whispered to me, "Watch him fall in." and we laughed to each other.

Derek unhooked the rope, retied it, and then ran fast to catch the dock before it was too far away for him to jump onto it. He leapt, but only landed halfway on the dock, grasping to pull himself up for a couple of seconds before completely falling off into the water.

As he rushed out of the water and back to the land dock, Sarah and I busted out laughing. He looked up at me, so I tried to stop laughing and squeezed out, "Are you okay?"

I could tell he was embarrassed, and probably mad at me for laughing at him, but I will never forget that moment because he handled it like a man. He didn't get mad or act like a jerk. He just climbed up from the water and kept quiet, his face blank, trying not to show any emotion. He was probably hoping I would forget it if he acted like nothing had happened. He looked so cute, standing there all dripping wet and embarrassed, that it made me fall for him even more.

After he dried off and changed clothes, he came back out and grilled us some burgers for dinner. As we sat and ate together, he asked me to go to the prom with him. He did it totally nonchalantly, like, "Hey, prom's next week. Do you want to go with me?"

I was so happy. I couldn't believe that Derek was asking me to the prom. I threw my arms around him and kissed him. "Of course, I want to go with you!" I was ecstatic. I liked him so much. Plus, it felt cool to be going to prom as a sophomore—very few sophomores are ever invited to Senior Prom.

After we finished eating, we cuddled on the couch. He held me really close and we lay there looking at each other. He was quiet for a little while and then he said, "You know, when we go to prom I really want to have sex. Are you okay with that? Everyone has sex that night. All the guys will make fun of me if we don't."

He had on such a puppy dog face that I couldn't help laughing, but my response was serious. "I'm not going to prom with you if you think you're getting sex that night. Just because everyone does it doesn't mean we have to. *If* we have sex, I want it to be special."

Derek gave me a sexy grin. "I *will* make it special."

That sounded so cheesy to me. I stuck to my guns. "No, Derek, sorry. If it's that important to you, go with someone else."

I was never afraid to let a boy go if he was pressuring me to do something I wasn't comfortable with—he could go do whatever he wanted with some other girl. At that point, it was up to Derek to make or break our relationship.

Derek looked at me for a moment and then whispered, "Okay, no pressure."

I was relieved. Truthfully, I was already feeling attached to him and didn't really want to let him go. But I also felt strongly that he had to prove how serious he was about me in order for us to be that intimate. I wasn't going to have sex for the first time with just any guy. It had to be someone I loved, and who I was sure loved me back. I wanted Derek to be that guy—I hoped that he would be—but I knew we weren't ready yet.

He was pretty quiet for the rest of the night. Obviously he wasn't used to rejection and my response had shocked him. I felt a little bad for him, but I figured he needed to start getting used to hearing the word "no." If he was going to date me, he wasn't always going to get his way.

# THE CROTCH INCIDENT

After that, we hung out every day that we didn't have school, work, or sports, and we would be on the phone for hours on the days we couldn't see each other. Friends weren't really a priority in those days. We just wanted to be with each other.

Derek was really showing that he cared about me and wanted to get to know me better. He would call me a lot, and take me out to dinner and to the movies. He seemed to really enjoy being with me. When he talked about his future he always included me as a part of it, like we would be dating for years to come. I felt so close to him.

Meanwhile, it was getting closer and closer to prom. I still hadn't really met his family, but I decided not to think about that and focused on getting ready. I ordered my prom dress online, which I knew was probably a bad idea, but I saw this dress that I just had to have. It was shiny hot pink with a haltered top and a low back that showed off my best asset at the time—my butt. Of course, when the dress came I totally didn't have enough boobage to fill it up.

Fortunately, I've since fixed that problem.

While I was trying to solve my cleavage dilemma, I asked Derek what he was going to wear. I wanted everything about prom night to be perfect. He told me he and his stepdad were going to go look at tuxedos and his dad was going to buy it for him as a birthday present. Our prom was on May 5th, Derek's birthday was May 8th, and my birthday was May 31st. May was going to be a big month for us and I was bursting with excitement.

Finally, it was the beginning of May and prom day was approaching fast. I had managed to get my dress problem sorted out, fortunately. I had to use two pairs of boob pads to fill out the top, but it looked pretty good. (I was a little nervous about making sure they stayed hidden, but I had my fingers crossed.) So, now I had the perfect dress, I had found the perfect shoes, and I had made appointments to get my makeup and hair done.

I was ready.

I called Derek to see if he wanted to do pictures at his house for his parents, but he said, "No."

I was shocked. For all the other dances I had gone to—which weren't nearly as big a deal as prom—both sets of parents, mine and the guy's, always wanted photos. Then he told me we *would* be stopping to do pictures at the houses of his friends with whom we were going. The fact that only Derek's family wasn't taking any pictures made me continue to wonder about his relationship with his parents. I didn't push him to explain, but it added to the mystery surrounding his family.

When prom night finally arrived, Derek showed up at my house to do pictures and met my parents together for the first time. He was in an all-white tux, looking perfect. The corsage he gave me was the perfect pink to match my dress. Little touches like that made me like him even more.

I was nervous about him meeting my parents, but you could tell Derek had it worse—he was sweating from nerves. It made me laugh, to see him so anxious, and it felt kind of good, since I knew he wouldn't be so nervous if he

didn't really like me and want to make a good impression on my parents.

After we posed for pictures outside, my parents told us to be safe and for me not to be out too late. Then off we went.

Our first stop was the house of one of the girls in our group, where I got to meet the other couples that would be with us.

I was the youngest in the group and it was a little awkward for me at first. Of all the couples, Derek and I had been dating for the least amount of time. The newness of our relationship made me feel a little out of place, but I wanted to ignore that and focus on having the night of my life.

Derek had made a deal with his sister to borrow her car for the night, so after more pictures we ended up going to Derek's house to switch cars and drop his sister off at her boyfriend's. It was a very strange experience; we stayed outside the whole time. I wasn't sure what was going on, but it seemed like Derek was avoiding his mother and stepfather. On any other night I could understand doing that, but on prom night? That seemed odd to me.

Derek's sister surprised me by asking to take pictures of me and Derek. I had gotten the impression from the first time we met that she didn't like me, but now I thought maybe I had read her wrong and she was good with me dating her brother after all. I felt like at least this was a positive sign that she was warming to me.

After we dropped Derek's sister off, we met our group of friends for dinner at a steak house. I totally enjoyed myself there. We all got along and had a great time and got to bond some more.

Then, suddenly, dinner was over and it was time for me to go to my first prom.

We arrived at the Mid-America Center, an enormous complex where they host everything from conventions and sporting events to proms and banquets. We took some fun photos in the entryway and said "hi" to everyone on the way in. It was like walking a red carpet—and I was Derek's leading lady.

We got in line for our prom picture and Derek chatted with his buddies, while I worried about my dress holding together and how we were going to pose.

Finally the photographer called us up. She asked me to be on one side and Derek on the other. She told me to pose a certain way and lean in, and she asked Derek to put his hand by my bellybutton.

And that's when everything got weird.

Derek put his hand on my crotch!

I'm still not sure if he put his hand there on purpose, but when it happened, it became obvious to me what was really on his mind and what he wanted at the end of the night. Everyone waiting in line saw. Our friends were laughing and Derek had turned bright pink from embarrassment.

I wasn't laughing. I was mad. I thought, *Derek's cool "no pressure" act and his claim to not want "anything" on prom night just went out the window.*

Derek knew he was busted, too. He kept giving me this puppy dog

"I'm sorry" look. To his friends, I played it off like I didn't think it was that big of a deal—I didn't want everyone knowing that he had embarrassed me—but I let Derek know I was annoyed. I couldn't let him think it was okay that he had touched my crotch in front of everyone. Then he might think he had a chance to have sex with me that night—and that totally was not in my plans.

After the crotch incident, we went and found our group and sat down at our table. We took more pictures with different friends. We danced, ate, and drank. Everybody was talking about After Prom and all the after parties—there were a lot of them going on.

Then it was time for the final dance—the Senior Dance. Derek and I shouldn't have been out on the dance floor, but our senior friends got us out there and it was one of those times in high school when you have to admit to yourself: *This is so damn great! I have the perfect date. I'm with the perfect group. I'm hanging with cool upperclassmen!*

It really was the ideal prom—one that I didn't want to end or to ever forget.

# AFTER PROM

As we were leaving, a dark cloud began to gather over my perfect, dreamy prom. When we were heading out, a couple of Derek's guy friends asked me, "Are you and Derek having sex?"

I was thinking, *It's none of your fucking business!* But I didn't want to be a bitch, so I bit my tongue and just said, "No way!"

Derek was standing right next to me when they asked, but he didn't say anything. I felt totally awkward and uncomfortable. I was sure that Derek had told them I had said "yes" to sex on prom night, so I asked him, "Have you said anything to your guy friends about our sex life?"

Maybe it shouldn't have been a big deal, but it felt like he had lied to me back when he had said, "no pressure," that day at Sarah's house. Now it seemed that by then he had apparently already told his friends that we would have sex on prom night.

Derek claimed that he hadn't said anything and acted like it was nothing to worry about. I didn't know what to believe, so I let it go.

We got ready to leave and when we walked outside it was pouring rain. Not just a few drops, or even a steady soaking rain—this was a torrential downpour. My heart sank. I couldn't believe it. I thought, *Prom night cannot end like this!*

Derek went and got the car and pulled it up for me so that I wouldn't get wet. He had gotten soaked walking to the car, so he decided we should go back to his house so he could change out of his tux.

I figured that when we got there his parents would be up and I could finally meet them. I was psyched to tell them all about how prom went and all about our night and give them all the details parents usually love to hear. That's what we would have done with my parents.

Instead, as we tried to dash through the rain into Derek's house, we were stopped abruptly at the front door. From the doorway, his mom and step-dad stared at us and there was this huge awkward silence. When they finally spoke, they asked us why we were there. I was so uncomfortable that I couldn't speak.

Derek said, "I have to change out of my tux. It's completely soaked."

We started walking to his room, but were stopped again. "She can wait right here," his mom said. I wondered if Derek might be in trouble with his mom. He hurried off to change and I just stood there in the doorway waiting in silence, while his mom and stepdad watched TV. When Derek came back he immediately said, "Let's go," so we just left.

As we were driving away, one of his friends called and said that their car got flooded and that they were trying to get it out. I turned to Derek. "I can totally believe their car got flooded!" It had been pouring so hard, I was sure that there would be flash floods in some places.

I asked Derek if he wanted to go to After Prom and do whatever lame activity had been set up for us, or if he wanted to call some friends to see where they were. I desperately wanted to salvage what was left of our night. He said that because of the rain, most of his friends had stayed at After Prom, but he clearly wasn't in the mood to do that.

Instead, he started driving to my house.

I felt sad that the rain had ruined our after-prom fun, so when he parked outside my house I told him he should come in until the rain stopped. I figured if my parents were up we could tell them the situation and they would understand.

My parents were already asleep, so we let ourselves in and ran upstairs to my bedroom so I could dry off and change and we could get comfy. I had already made it clear that we were not having sex, so I figured it would be like all the other nights Derek and I had hung out in my room and he hadn't tried anything.

I went to the bathroom to change and came back to lie down with Derek, snuggle up, and get some sleep. But he said, "I can't sleep."

I was exhausted, but I turned to him and mumbled, "Okay. Let's talk then."

Derek took my hand. "Can we please try having sex? I promise it will be special. This is our first prom together…Please."

I just looked at him.

"*Please?*" Derek wheedled. "It can be my birthday present."

When I didn't say anything, he changed tactics. He started making out with me and going below the belt with his hands.

He was fighting dirty. My body felt amazing and he was turning me on by doing this thing with his tongue in my ear.

Then he whispered, "Let's just try it and I'll stop if it hurts you."

In the end it wasn't the pressure from his friends or even from him. I was just so turned on that I totally caved. "Okay," I said. "But let's not do it in my bed, let's go to the front bedroom. My bed is too small." It was a twin and I thought it would be better if we had more room.

So we went to the front guest bedroom. I had only a shirt on and Derek was naked. He lay down and said, "Get on top."

I assumed the position and tried to go for it, but it felt like I was stuck on a branch. It hurt so much. I tried easing myself down more slowly, but that didn't work either. Derek was huge and this was my first time. He encouraged me to keep trying and I did, but it just wasn't happening. We tried it with him on top, but it still hurt. I wasn't prepared for this much pain at two AM. We tried a few other random positions, but enough was enough. I just wasn't ready.

Derek finally spoke up. "Are you okay babe? If it's hurting too bad, we'll stop. I want you to enjoy it, too."

I spoke up quickly, through my pain, "Yeah, we need to be done." I was a little embarrassed because I was sure this wasn't exactly the hot after-prom sex Derek had envisioned, but at least we had tried.

We stopped and went back to my bedroom. He kissed me as we were falling asleep and said, "I'm happy we tried it."

I said I was, too, but really I was freaking out. I had all these thoughts racing through my head as I drifted off: *I just had sex...I just had sex in my house...I just had sex and it was nothing like what I thought it would be like... Derek better not break up with me now that we've had sex...Derek better not tell anyone we had sex...I need to get Derek out of the house before my parents wake up and find out we had sex...Oh my God, I just had SEX!*

When we woke up a few hours later, my first thought was that I wasn't a virgin anymore. It felt like I now had a huge secret to hide. I snuck Derek out through the front door (it was easier for him to go out that way because no one in my family ever used the front door) and then my parents woke up.

I tried to act like nothing big had happened the night before. I told them all about prom—the dinner, the pictures, the dancing—and they were happy for me. All they asked was what time I got home. I told them I got home early because of the rain, which was actually the truth. I was relieved they weren't more suspicious, but a little surprised, too. I was convinced anyone could read my face and know that I had had sex.

It's funny how something can happen that makes you feel completely different, but the change happens on the inside so no one else can see it.

# NOT LIKE A VIRGIN

———— ··◄◅∞▻►·· ————

The Sunday after prom, we celebrated Derek's birthday. I gave him presents and we hung out the whole day. We went out to dinner and a movie, and then I snuck him back to my house and we had sex again. It went much smoother this time.

School started up again on Monday. Since, Derek and I went to different high schools, none of my friends had been at his prom. All my girlfriends were asking to see pictures and wanted to know what had happened at the end of the night. They all asked, "So, did you have sex with Derek?" I didn't tell the truth. I couldn't. I just said "no" to everyone because I was terrified someone would tell my parents. Immediately after school I called Derek to make sure he hadn't told anyone that we had had sex. He said he hadn't, but that all the guys had been asking him about it.

My friends must have sensed I was lying, because they kept asking me if I had slept with Derek. They would not let it drop. Eventually, they wore me down and I gave up and told them the truth. Derek must have told his friends, too, because by the time we went out to a party the following weekend, everyone knew.  They pretended that they didn't, but I could tell by the way people were asking that they already knew the answer. Derek gave himself away, too, because around me he acted like the respectful boyfriend, but around his friends he was acting like "The Man," all cocky and grinning from ear to ear.

After our less than ideal introduction on prom night, the next time I met Derek's parents was a couple of weeks later when he invited me to his sister's graduation party at his house. I remember it being a little awkward and that I didn't feel totally comfortable. I didn't want Derek to feel bad so I brushed it off and we just did our own thing at the party.  We mostly hung out with his uncle and grandma, who were very welcoming and friendly to me.

We sat, eating and joking around, at our own table. I was talking to Derek's grandmother about not having enough boobs to fill out my prom dress because earlier she had commented that we looked great in our prom picture. Suddenly Derek said, "Then we should have a baby. That would make your boobs bigger." I laughed like it was a joke, but inside I was like, *He's thinking about us having children together?* I started thinking that marriage and a family might be a possibility for our future.

Meanwhile, though, Derek told me that his mom wasn't happy with us dating. I don't know if that was true, but I tried my best to act like everything was normal between his parents and me. Sometimes, when I called his home or even his cell phone, his mom would answer. I got the feeling that she didn't like me very much. After a while, it got so awkward that I just gave up calling Derek. I decided that if he wanted to speak to me, he would have to call me.

# HAPPY BIRTHDAY TO ME

My birthday was coming up and I was finally going to celebrate my Sweet Sixteen. I couldn't wait. Plus, school would be over soon and then Derek and I could spend all summer together. I was looking forward to us having more time to be together.

The night before my birthday, Derek and I went out. Later, I snuck him into my house to spend the night. We had sex (by now it didn't hurt anymore and we were getting pretty good at it) and then he left early in the morning, before my parents woke up. Then I had to hurry and get ready to go out with my family for my birthday. We were going out for brunch and then going to the zoo in the afternoon.

When I came back home from brunch, before the zoo, I found a big vase filled with beautiful red roses in my room on top of the TV and a note that said, *Happy Birthday! Love, Derek*. At first I was freaked out because I didn't know how the roses got there. Then I figured out that Derek must have left the front door unlocked when he left in the morning and then come back and put them in my room. I was impressed that he had come up with such a crafty plan and decided it was the most romantic gift I had ever received from a guy.

Later, after the zoo, while I was getting ready to go out to dinner and a party with my girlfriends, I called Derek to invite him to join us. That's when the fighting began. Derek flew off the handle because he wanted to take me to dinner alone. He threw a jealous fit and said he wasn't coming to dinner. He told me to just call him afterward and hung up on me.

I tried to shrug off the fight and went downtown with my girlfriends. I had a great time, but I wanted to spend my birthday with Derek, too. I tried to call him when we were done with dinner, but he wouldn't pick up his phone. I figured he was still pissed off, so the girls and I went to a couple of places to hang out, and then I dropped some of them off.

By that point it was getting kind of late and I wanted to hook up with Derek, so I texted one of his best friends, who was having a party at his house. I figured Derek was probably there and decided to head over there with my girl-friends. By the time we got there the party was winding down. There weren't that many people left and beer was the main beverage (which we didn't drink), so my girlfriends and I were ready to bail.

Then I found Derek.

He was with some random girl who was sitting on his lap.

I had run into a bunch of his guy friends who were roaming around the party, but they hadn't even tried to stop me from walking in on Derek. My instinct was to blame the girl and think she had pushed herself on Derek (I don't know if that was the case here or not), but he didn't even say "hi" to me or try to cover up what he had done.

I was speechless. I wouldn't have known what to do if my girls hadn't been there with me. I was so angry I just froze. I could have stood there and stared in shock for the rest of the night.

I was furious, but I figured we would talk about it and then he would apologize. I knew he was mad about my birthday and just trying to get back at me, but when I tried to talk to him he wouldn't leave his friends so we could talk alone. I couldn't believe how Derek was treating me—on my birthday! After everything I had done for him. I had been there for him on his birthday, and this was what I was getting in return?

My friends and I left because I couldn't take Derek being mean to me anymore. All I could think on the way home was, *I can't believe I had sex with someone like that.*

I tried to call him the next day, but he didn't pick up. When I finally talked to him the day after, he told me that he had decided that he didn't want to date during the summer.

I'm not going to lie: I was devastated. But I didn't want him to know how much he had hurt me. So I swallowed how crushed I was and responded, "Okay. That's fine. Talk to you at the end of the summer."

I was heartbroken, but I was also furious. How could Derek treat me like that? I wanted to do something to get back at him. I wanted to hurt him as much as he had hurt me.

It was going to be a very interesting summer.

# FLIRTING FOR REVENGE

Summer started and I was still boiling over with anger and jealousy. I wanted Derek to hear about me every weekend, every day, all the time. I wanted him to call me in the worst way. I wanted him to tell me that he had made a mistake. That he still needed me and wanted us to start dating again.

Only he didn't call.

So I would call him—for sex. Strictly sex. I acted like I didn't care about him in any other way. I was partying every night now. If my parents wanted me to stay home, I snuck out. I snuck Derek into my house, too, when he showed up for my booty call.

But the booty calls weren't enough. I wanted to be on Derek's mind even when he didn't want me to be. I wasn't letting anything get in the way of my goal. I would party all the time and flirt with all the guys I met, hoping Derek was hearing all about it.

At the time it seemed almost like a game, but in reality I was a little out of control. Normally, I never went out of my way to flirt with guys, but now I was flirting with a vengeance. I wanted to make the gossip "headlines" to be sure that Derek heard about me. The partying was getting to the point of distraction. I was out late at night so much, I started sleeping during the day. I felt like an owl.

Then, one night, I went a little too far. The flirting turned into making out, which almost turned into something else. This gossip "headline" did make it all the way to Derek, which I loved, but I also scared myself a little.

It was at a bonfire party. During the summer, lots of our friends would have bonfire parties out in the country. They were the hype of our summers— the smoky, woodsy smell, the crush of people all thronged intimately around the fire, being out in the open air and the feeling of freedom it gave you. They were always fun, and this one was especially fun—though, in the end, maybe too much fun.

I went with some girlfriends. We drove twenty minutes down a gravel road, the music up, singing like we were pop stars, texting fifty people at one time, hoping we didn't hit a deer.

We got there and parked the car in the huge line up of other cars, popped the caps of our UV blues and pinks, and downed them until we were tipsy. We ran through the high grass, smelled the smoke of the bonfire, saw the fiery light from the flames and the shadows of people leaning against the trees.

Now that we were there, it was as if the party had finally gotten started. We took over—flirting with the foreign exchange boys there for the summer, watching the guys compete over who could hop over the flames and not get burned, smoking weed in beer-can bongs, peeing in the grass and hang-drying, making out with whomever in the woods or in cars.

I drank way too much, so much that I had blurred double vision. I found myself in a truck, making out with some boy and calling him Derek. He was going below the belt and I started yelling, "Let's have sex!"

A friend came over and grabbed me out of the truck. "You idiot! That's not Derek!" she yelled. "Come on, we're leaving!"

I was so drunk I couldn't walk, so she had some boys carry me up the hill through the tall grass. I don't even remember getting home that night.

# I ROLL THE DICE

The next day my friend called and said, "So the boy you were making out with last night really likes you."

I laughed. "Oh my God! I can't believe I thought he was Derek. I honestly don't even remember what the guy looks like."

Then she asked, "Well, do you want to meet him? He wants to hang out with you."

I had nothing to lose. Derek wasn't calling me. So I thought, *Why not?* After all, Derek was acting like he wasn't interested and this guy definitely was into me. Plus, it was a chance to make Derek jealous.

So I met up with Bonfire Guy. He was nice enough, and I could tell he was very into me, but the whole time I was with him I couldn't stop thinking about how he wasn't Derek. I just wanted Derek. So I decided to take a huge gamble to win him back.

I hadn't talked to Derek in over a week, but I took a deep breath and called to ask him to come over so we could talk. I was actually a little embarrassed and ashamed of what I was going to do. I was planning to tell him about this other guy to make him jealous. I rationalized that it would show him how much I liked him, but also that I didn't care about him when I went out and had fun. Looking back, I can see how ridiculous my plan was, but at the time I was stuck. I wanted Derek back and I didn't know what else to do.

In the end, it went down like this: It was a perfect summer afternoon and I was waiting outside on my front porch. Derek drove up and parked right outside our gate. I was nervous but so happy to see him. As Derek opened the gate, I said, "Hi."

He looked me over, playing it very cool. "Hey. So…you wanted to tell me something?"

At this point in our relationship (or non-relationship) I could tell he wore the pants high and proud, and I was tired of him acting like it. I wanted to shake him up a little. I took a deep breath and plunged right in, saying everything all in a rush.

"So the other night, I went out with the girls. I drank too much and ended up making out with some boy. I barely even remember what he looks like, so it really doesn't matter, but I wanted to tell you so I wouldn't be hiding anything from you."

I paused to catch my breath and then added, "I understand if you don't want to talk to me anymore, but at least I told you."

When I was done, Derek was quiet. He didn't even look at me. The silence ate at me and I realized that maybe I had truly messed up. I looked down at the ground and stayed like that, not saying anything more. I had rolled the dice and come up a loser.

I heard Derek say, "I gotta go."

I didn't look up. I couldn't. "Bye," I said almost to myself.

In my mind, it had been a straight shot from "we are so perfect and cute" to "he doesn't care about me at all." I felt like a month ago we had been so happy and in love and now here he was walking away. I couldn't believe it was ending like this. I felt so stupid.

I looked up in time to see him shut the gate. Then I turned and fixed my eyes on my house so I wouldn't have to see him leave. I would just hear his car start up and then I would know that he was leaving.

But I didn't hear the car start. Instead, I heard Derek's footsteps as he came back up on the porch with a big smile on his face. I looked up at him and he said, "I like you too much to stop seeing you. But don't do it again!" I smiled back at him and we hugged each other close for a long time and then he had to leave to go to work. I was thrilled that Derek had finally admitted how much he liked me.

Gradually, we fell back into being boyfriend and girlfriend again. We started doing everything as a couple again, like I had been wanting, and he shared everything with me—or so it seemed at the time. But something had definitely changed. The trust between us had been damaged and we could never quite get back to the way we had been.

Partly, it was that I needed to let him know why I had kissed some-one else. I wanted to talk about everything that had happened between us. But somehow the time never seemed right to talk about it, so it all went unsaid.

I still thought about it, though. Inside, I knew it had happened because Derek had not really been my boyfriend and that had hurt. I had lost control at the bonfire party because I had wanted Derek to be there with me, as my boy-friend, the way it used to be. Instead, he had been at some other party, doing his own thing. Derek never told me if he had kissed anyone else or if he was flirting with someone else that night, or that summer for that matter, and I never asked.

Still, even though important things went unsaid, I was happy that we were seeing each other again for more than just booty calls, so I concentrated on that. Despite what he had said earlier, Derek had discovered that he couldn't live without me.

Meanwhile, Bonfire Guy apparently hadn't been as drunk that night as

I had been. He kept pestering my girlfriends, asking to hang out with me. One day his crew of guys showed up where I was hanging out with my girlfriends and we met again. After that, they kept showing up until we finally agreed to start hanging out with them. He would invite me to his friends' parties where I knew my girlfriends would be. I told him that Derek and I were dating again but it was cool if he and I were just friends.

This caused some friction at parties and it was definitely a juggling act for me, but I didn't mind because that crew of guys was nice and I loved the attention. But Derek definitely did not think the situation was so cute. Now that we were back to going out instead of just having sex, he was getting jealous and possessive.

I started thinking I had gambled and won after all. Somehow I had played the game right. I thought, *I have the boy I want and now he's all mine.*

# THE LYING STARTS

—••◦◦✲◦◦••—

Derek and I continued our late night intimacy and our growing relationship through the beginning of July. Then, over the July 4th holiday weekend, Shelly had a party at her house and kids from every high school in our district were there.

I went to the party without Derek. He said he would stop by early and bring me food, but he couldn't stay because he had to go help his stepdad with some work. His stepfather was a truck driver and Derek would help him from time to time. Shelly found it weird that he was going to work on a holiday night, but I defended him and insisted that it wasn't so strange.

Derek showed up with my favorite Jimmy John's sandwich. Some of my friends were inside the house and the rest were outside by the lake. We could hear a lot of people outside on the deck, but we were enjoying our time together inside, chatting and sharing my sandwich.

Derek was a little unhappy because Bonfire Guy and his crew were at the party and he had to leave to go help his stepdad, but I just hugged him to show him that he was the only one I cared about. Then I told him, "Let's go up-stairs and you can help me finish getting ready." Derek was always good about watching me get ready. He liked to watch me put my makeup on—it made me feel so sexy and beautiful.

We went upstairs and hung out and talked while I got ready. Afterwards, on the way out of the room, I grabbed his manhood and dared him to stick it in right then and there. We were both laughing because we knew we could only go about a second without being seen. But he did it and, *Oh my God!*

Then we heard people downstairs, coming in from the deck. If they looked up, they would have seen us doing it on the landing, so instead I switched to licking him down south. Now I was hidden so it looked like he was just standing upstairs on his own. It was fun and sneaky and left Derek a little on the spot, as he had to pretend that nothing was happening while being totally teased by me. He started laughing because we were so about to get caught.

I heard someone downstairs ask, "Where's Farrah?" I didn't really want to get caught, so I stood up and said, "Okay, let me walk you outside."

As we walked downstairs and outside some of my girlfriends followed us to the front of the house to watch us kiss and say goodbye. We really got into it. It was probably quite a show. For me it was the sexiest way a guy could say goodbye to me.

I said, "I'm going to miss you. Call me if you get done helping your stepdad early."

Derek smiled at me. "Okay, I will. Don't flirt with any boys."

We were staring into each other's eyes, talking to each other so close, our hips connected as we rocked from side to side. It felt sexy and right. I turned to leave and Derek tapped my booty "bye" and my girlfriends' jaws all dropped. One of my friends joked, "Ooh, your hips were rockin'!" There were giggles and winks all around and I thought, *Aww, I have my perfect boyfriend.*

Two days later, Derek and I went on a dinner date to a restaurant where he used to work. I was trying to enjoy myself, but Derek was being such a jerk that I couldn't. There wasn't much to our conversation, and he seemed to be checking out some girl who worked there. I couldn't understand why he was acting that way. Then one of the servers approached our table. He was apparently friends with Derek.

"How's your food?" he asked.

I said, "Fine, thanks."

Then he said to Derek, "Good seeing you at that party the other night. That was a crazy Fourth of July!"

...*Blah, blah, blah* he went on, but I zoned out and just looked up at this guy and then over at Derek. Derek's face had turned red. Busted.

I was so shocked and angry I could barely speak, but I managed to say, "You went out the other night?"

The guy looked over at Derek, realizing he'd ratted his friend out. Then he laughed and walked away.

Derek just sat there, not acting like such a jerk anymore.

I looked at him, waiting for an explanation.

Finally he said, "I got done helping my stepdad early."

At this point, I was fuming. "You couldn't have told me that yesterday?" Obviously, Derek had wanted to go party with other people on the Fourth from the get-go. Or maybe he had gotten a better offer. Either way, he hadn't been straight with me about where he was that night.

When I thought back to how clueless I had been at the party, how I had flirted and fooled around with him before he went off to supposedly go work with his stepfather, I got more and more angry. I sat there fuming, staring out the window.

Derek acted cocky about it, trying to laugh and play it off like it didn't matter. But the only thing I could laugh about was how dumb he must have thought I was. I refused to eat the rest of my dinner and felt a little satisfaction that he had to pay for it anyway. I wanted to waste his money on purpose, like he had wasted my time by not being honest with me.

# THE GREEN-EYED MONSTER REARS IT'S UGLY HEAD

Of course, I forgave Derek. I liked him too much not to. After that, we started getting closer and closer and it felt like things were getting more serious between us. Summer was winding down and we were determined to party as much as possible. We loved hanging out with our friends. It was like our friends were our family and our families were just our landlords.

One night Derek and I went to a party at a friend's apartment. We were having a good time, but then this girl showed up who was always trying to hang out with Derek. Even though all my girlfriends knew how into each other Derek and I were and would always mention how Derek looked at me and was there for me, I was still a little insecure. I'm a confident person, but that image of Derek with that girl sitting on his lap on my birthday was now burned into my brain.

I turned into a jealous, overprotective monster.

Normally, I was more into chilling and having fun, but when someone you're dating has a girl getting closer and closer and that girl keeps avoiding you, you know something's up. You feel like she will go behind your back and have your boyfriend sneak right back there with her.

I had lost my virginity to Derek and felt like sex had turned our relationship into something pretty serious. I didn't need some girl ruining everything. So when it looked to me like she was starting to flirt with him, I yelled, straight up, "Stay the fuck away from Derek! I'll kick your ass!"

All of a sudden the party atmosphere stopped and the guys made a barrier between the two of us. I had taken it too far. In the end, the girl left, but then his friends said that I couldn't be coming out if I was going to start fights. I had nothing to say to that, because I had been the one to start the fight.

It was very out of character for me to act like that. I never used to say one word to a boy I was dating if he had girls around him. But sleeping with Derek had changed me. Sex is a big step in a relationship. It should be for when people are in love. We weren't in love yet (or at least we hadn't admitted it to each other) and I didn't want anything—or anyone—ruining the chances of us falling in love.

# CLOSE CALL

At first Derek seemed flattered that I had fought for him, but after that he didn't want to go out together as much anymore. I assumed it was because his friends were worried I might start another fight. We started going out separately more and more, but we would always meet up back at my place and he would spend the night.

Derek was like my best friend, my boyfriend, and my lover all in one, and I loved partying and hanging out and cozying up in bed with him. Sometimes if I fell asleep before he came over he would chuck a pencil or piece of mulch up at my window to get my attention to let him in. He was like my Romeo. By the end of summer, the roof by my window had a big collection of random objects.

My mom questioned me one day about it. "Farrah, I saw by your window there was mulch, pens, pencils, rocks up on the roof." I waved it off, "It's probably from our weird neighbors. Or maybe the wind blew it up there." Surprisingly, she left it alone after that.

But one night that summer we came really close to getting caught.

Derek and I had overslept one morning and when Derek woke up he heard my dad coming down the hall. I felt him jump off the bed. Then he ran and hid in my closet and shut the door.

My dad came in my room and said, "Good morning. It's time to get up and get ready for the day."

I was so terrified, I just said, "Okay, get out of here and I will."

After my dad left, I got up and opened my closet door and Derek and I busted out laughing. I whispered, "I need to get you out of here!" When we could her my parents in the kitchen cooking breakfast, I snuck Derek out the front door and whispered, "Call me later."

Phew!

# LUV U BABE

The first time Derek told me he loved me was on August 11, 2007. He sent me a message on Myspace. He wrote, "i really really love u babe" and that he wasn't sure if I felt the same way. He hoped I did, but he couldn't hold it in any longer and had to tell me how he felt.

I saved all our messages. Now I'm so glad I did.

Even now I still try to remember everything about the day he sent me that message. It meant so much to me that he wrote to me he loved me, but never asked for, or expected, an "I love you back" out of me. That's when you know that a person's love for you is genuine. They don't want anything from you; they just have to tell you how they feel because they can't hold it inside any longer.

Seeing that message made all the ups and downs of our relationship worth it. All that time spent waiting for him to call, all the lies, and the not always hanging out with me—it made it all worth it.

It's crazy how you can see things through rose-colored glasses when you want to. It seems like the consequence of having sex is that even if you haven't been with that person very long you try to stay with that person. You try to find fulfillment in a relationship with that person because you have shared the most intimate thing you can share with them. Your main goal is to reach love and happiness with them. You overlook the relationship deal-breakers. You act like truly devastating moments don't even matter. Especially when he is the first.

# CAUGHT IN THE ACT

Derek and I kept mastering the art of the sneak in, until one night it all came crashing to a horrible end...

One evening in August, Derek and I were checking in with each other on the phone and I asked him what he was doing later that night.

He said, "Let's hang out tonight. I'll come over."

I told him, "My mom and dad aren't going to let anyone come over because my mom is out of town for work."

"No problem," Derek said. "I'll just sneak in, stay 'til the morning, and then sneak back out."

That sounded like a good plan (in fact, it was our usual plan) so I told him to call me around 9:00 and I would let him know if the coast was clear.

When he called, he was already at my house.

I checked to make sure my dad was asleep and then went to meet Derek at the front door. We ran up the front staircase together, went into my bedroom, shut the door, and were like, *Yes! We made it!*

We always had a great time hanging out in my room together and that night was no exception. We were talking and watching TV and generally having fun. Then Derek wanted to mix things up and decided we should have sex in my sister's room down the hall. (My sister wasn't home, just FYI.) I told Derek that we needed to be super quiet because my dad would be up soon.

We went to her room and had sex on the bed for a good hour. At one point Derek was on top of me and I looked up at him and noticed a light a little bit to the side of his head, but off in the distance. I was about to say, "What is that?" but before I had a chance, Derek flew off of me and the overhead light turned on. I grabbed two big pillows to cover my naked body and looked up to see my dad. He was as angry as I have ever seen him.

I was in shock and all I could bring myself to say was, "Michael what are you doing? Get out of here!"

My dad didn't answer. He wasn't going anywhere.

Derek stood up from the floor by the other side of the bed, still naked. My dad glared at him and said, "Get dressed, Derek, and come downstairs. We're going to call your mom."

Then he walked out of the room.

I felt so bad for Derek. He looked scared and nervous. I asked him, "What's your mom going to say?"

Fumbling to put his clothes back on, he said, "I'm probably going to get in trouble and have my car taken away."

Then he went downstairs to talk to my dad. I thought about going down with him, but I was worried that my being there would just make things worse. It was late and I knew that I was in for some big trouble in the morning, so I went to sleep.

Looking back, it probably would have been better if I had gone downstairs with Derek, because then maybe things wouldn't have happened the way they did.

The next morning when I finally came downstairs, my dad looked as if he hadn't gotten any sleep. He wouldn't look at me—he was that angry. I was thankful, at least, that my mom was out of town and I wouldn't have to face her wrath, too.

But then my dad said, "I called your mom. She's going to call you later. We decided you're going to go stay at your grandparent's house for a while." I didn't say anything. I just went back up to my room. I was furious. I didn't want to go to my grandparents, where I wasn't allowed to do anything.

I called some friends and invited them over. We sat upstairs in my room talking over the whole situation. I begged them to stay with me all day so I wouldn't have to be at home alone with my dad. They felt bad for me and agreed that my parents were wrong to send me away to my grandparents.

That evening my mom called. She said she would talk to me more when she got home from her business trip the next day, but that I was going to have to go stay at my grandparents after that. I told her I wasn't going, but I knew I wasn't going to win this battle.

When my mom finally got home the next day, my dad acted like he was the victim of a crime. I knew that it was a big deal to them, but Derek and I had talked before my mom came home and he had said, "Your parents are over-reacting. Everyone has sex."

I thought they were being totally unfair, but when we all finally sat down at the dining room table to discuss the situation, my dad dropped a bombshell. "Derek and his mom went to the police station and filed a report. They're pressing charges against me for hitting Derek."

I was in shock. First of all, I didn't even know that my dad had hit Derek. He hadn't mentioned anything to me about it and he had seemed completely fine when we talked. Which was a little strange, given that it seemed like he and his mom were now trying to get my dad in trouble with the police.

My mom went on, "Farrah, do you think it's okay that you snuck your boyfriend in here and had Michael catch you two having sex and now Michael might have to go to jail?"

I knew I couldn't win with that question, so I kept quiet.

"You're going to your grandma's," my mom went on, "Until we figure out what we're going to do. You can stay there until school starts and you won't have your phone and you are not going out."

I was pissed. Pissed at them for punishing me so harshly and pissed at Derek for not telling me the whole story. I felt like I had been ambushed. I ran upstairs and called Derek. He picked up, acting like everything was great. Well, things weren't great.

"You're trying to get my dad in trouble!" I yelled at him.

"Your dad hit me," Derek replied.

"Yeah, because you snuck into his house and had sex with me! It's your fault, Derek, and now I have to go to my grandma's for the rest of summer and I can't bring my phone. You better not go out while I'm grounded and stuck at my grandparents."

Derek reminded me that my parents were overreacting. He added, "But I won't go out while you're grounded, I'll wait for your call. I love you."

I said, "I love you, too," and hung up.

# LOCK-DOWN AT GRANDMA AND GRANDPA'S

My parents made it clear that I had no choice but to go stay with my grandparents. I was still furious about it and did a lot of yelling, but they wouldn't budge.

So the next day I ended up at my grandma's house.

My days there consisted of being bored out of my mind inside the house and being bored out of my mind walking around outside. I was allowed to go to work, but that was it. I didn't have my phone and I wasn't allowed to go out and party.

At the time I was working at a Hy-Vee supermarket, and one day when I was outside bringing some shopping carts in, I ran into a friend whom I hadn't seen since he graduated.

He invited me to go out that weekend, but I said I couldn't. I told him the shortened version of what had happened with me and Derek and how I was in lock-down at my grandparents.

My friend looked surprised. "Well, I think I met your boyfriend the other night," he told me. He said he had gone to a party and met some of my girlfriends, who had a guy with them, who had to have been Derek. He said they had all been talking about how much they missed me and wished I was there.

While I was happy I was being missed and mentioned, I was mad that Derek went out to a party (with *my* friends) while I was stuck in Hell because of him. I had believed him when he said he wouldn't go out without me, but I should have known better.

Back at my grandparents after work that night, I went online and, yep, there were all the photos posted from the night Derek went out with my girlfriends. The whole thing just made me burn. I couldn't take it anymore.

I picked up my grandparent's phone and called Derek, and when he answered I told him that I had heard that he had gone out to a party, and that I saw the photos online.

"Why are you going out when I can't?" I asked him. "I'm in this trouble because of you!"

He said that he missed me a lot, but that he didn't want to just sit at home. Then he told me to call him every night. I felt a little better. At least he had been out with my friends and not with other girls. And, to be honest, I don't know if I would have been able to stay home while he was grounded.

So I stopped being mad and called him every night and just kept hoping that my parents would cool down and let me come home and go out again.

# FREE AT LAST!

---•‹∞›•---

After three hellish weeks at my grandparents—three weeks of not having my phone and not being able to go out or see Derek—my mom called one day and told me, "We're going to family counseling on Sunday."

I said, "Fine," but inside I was like, *Oh my God, my parents can't deal with anything. They're so dramatic.* I was sure that the counselor would take their side and that my punishment would go on and on and I was dreading the whole experience.

Sunday came and we all went to the counselor's. I was ready to go on the defensive, but to my surprise, the whole experience was very positive. The office was serene and quiet and the counselor was actually very cool. She made me feel at ease and I had no problem talking to her. My parents, on the other hand, seemed very uptight and very angry.

The counselor wanted to hear from my parents first, so I listened while they talked. It was mainly my mom talking and she shared how they felt about Derek and me and everything she said seemed so negative. Listening to her made me feel like there was no hope. The way she was talking, I thought they might decide to send me away to a halfway house for troubled teens or, worse, leave me at my grandparents forever.

Finally the counselor said it was my turn to talk. I told her about my relationship with Derek and said that I wanted to be able to date him still. She made me feel so understood that I got brave and said I wanted to switch schools so that I could go to school with Derek.

Shockingly, the counselor was on my side! My parents were mad, but they had agreed to listen to her. She did bring up valid points of concern, such as maintaining my grades and respecting my curfew and my parents' rules. No more sneaking around or sneaking Derek into my bedroom, but basically she said that I should be allowed to still date Derek and to go to school with him if I wanted.

Before we left the session, we agreed to some basic rules and a curfew, which meant that I would be able to leave my grandparent's and come back home. Life was definitely getting better. I also got my phone back. I called Derek right away and told him the good news. He was happy and asked if I wanted to go out the coming weekend before school started.

My parents had given me a curfew of midnight, and I didn't want them to get mad at me again, so when Derek picked me up that weekend I told him we had to make sure I got home in time. He totally understood. He didn't want to rock the boat, either.

We drove out to a party at a friend's house in the country. There was grass and stars for miles all around. We hung out in the house and drank, talking to all of our friends who were about to start college. Derek and his buddies did a couple of beer bongs, but then it was getting late and I wanted some alone time with Derek, so I said, "Let's go outside."

Derek told his buddies we were going outside so that no one would bother us. It was perfect! We claimed our sex life back on the hood of his car and I looked at him and all the millions of stars in the sky and I will never forget how perfect it felt.

Best of all, Derek dropped me off at home on time for curfew.

# BACK TO SCHOOL

The next week we went back to school. The first few days were all about class schedules and getting school pictures taken. You have to wait in long lines for everything and there are so many students that the line for registration starts trailing outside the building.

I was excited to be starting at a new school, especially since I was going to be able to see Derek during the school day now. I didn't anticipate, however, that us being at the same school would put me in some pretty awkward situations. But I found that out on the very first day back.

My parents were with me waiting in line to pay for registration and make sure I was enrolled in the right classes and sports. I looked up and saw Derek and his mother and stepfather ahead of us in line. My parents hadn't noticed, so I slowed them down to keep us from running into them. I figured that after everything that had happened that summer it would be best to keep our families apart. After Derek's mom pressed charges against my dad, my parents wanted nothing to do with his family.

I kept my parents' attention focused on my registration forms, but I kept sneaking glances at Derek and his mother and stepfather. From what I could tell, it seemed like they were just going through the motions of registration. They looked bored and Derek seemed like he wanted to bail as soon as possible.

I did my best to keep my parents from noticing Derek and his family, but I couldn't keep it up for long. Eventually, my mom and dad got really quiet, it seemed like everything went quiet, and I could tell they had seen Derek ahead of us in line. So there I was with my mom and dad, pretending that my boyfriend wasn't in the same line—pretending that I didn't even know him. It was ridiculous, but I didn't want there to be a scene or an embarrassing situation in the auditorium, before I'd even had my first class.

Fortunately, by the time we were about halfway through the line, Derek was at the front and then I saw him leave. The tension broke and I was relieved. It was insane to not even be able to say "hi" to my boyfriend on our first day of school. But things had escalated out of control so quickly; I didn't even know what normal was anymore.

Once the school year started and our parents weren't around, things got better. Derek and I shared a locker and walked to classes together. We were the hottest couple in school and all of his exes were jealous.

I loved every moment of it.

Derek would pick me up for school at 7:00 AM on Mondays, even though our classes didn't start until 9:30 AM. We would go to his house, because his mom was at work (at the time she was a manager at a truck stop) and Derek would cook me breakfast. Then we'd have sex in the kitchen, or the shower, or even his mom's room.

We had no shame.

Or, sometimes, we would just hang out and play with his new puppy, Tutty. I loved every second, because it felt like how it would be if Derek and I lived together. We fantasized about getting our own place and living together and it felt like it was just a matter of time before that would happen.

After school, if I had to cheer at a game, we would go to his mom's house to hang out first. I would change into my uniform and be his personal cheerleader right there on the couch. His sisters didn't seem to like how affectionate we were. They complained that we were too loud and wanted us to stay in his room more. Derek would make fun of them. I thought it was funny, and

I didn't mind their complaints as long as they didn't make problems for us.

We spent hours in his room and after we had sex he would take pictures of us. He acted so crazy about me. He had our prom pictures in his room and my number written on his wall, as well as the numbers of my closest girlfriends—that way, if his mom got angry and took his phone, he could still get in touch with me.

Sometimes he would pick me up and put us against his mirror and say, "We look like models. We're so hot together."

I thought so, too.

Then his mom would come home and ruin our fun. Derek would hear her come in and we worried that we were going to get in trouble.

I felt like she didn't like me and I couldn't figure out why. I didn't feel

I just wanted to be with my boyfriend and forget about parents and rules, so sometimes Derek and I would skip school on half-days. A lot of my girlfriends did that, too, and honestly junior year of high school was so easy I was able skip school without ever falling behind.

# NO PROMISES

———•·◄∞►·•———

Things were great between Derek and I in the fall, but high school relationships are roller coasters—and I do not like to ride roller coasters.

Around December, things started to go really wrong. It was that time before Christmas break when no one is getting much schoolwork done and everyone is just coasting into the holiday vacation. One day, Derek and I were walking hand-in-hand down the hallway and I started talking about this girl in my class who had just told me that one of Derek's friends had given her a promise ring. I was shocked because they hadn't been dating that long. I said, "We've been dating longer than most of these couples and you don't see us with rings. I think it's crazy."

Derek smiled and said, "Yeah."

I was waiting for him to follow up with, "…it's way too soon to be thinking about those things." But he just said, "Yeah," and left it at that. It was like I was the only one who thought that having an engagement ring at fifteen or sixteen was crazy. We were all still so young. I cared about Derek and I wanted us to have that kind of future, but a voice in my head was yelling, *Whoa, way to soon!*

Of course, I thought it would be great if one day Derek gave me a promise ring or an engagement ring, maybe in a year or two, but I was proud that we were being serious about our relationship and taking our time. I talked about how I thought a promise ring was a big responsibility, but I was really trying to send him the message: *Do not give me a ring yet. We're not ready.*

We already had too many issues that made me unsure of our future. First and foremost, if we were truly going to have a future together, I felt we needed our families to learn to be more supportive of our relationship. I wanted so badly for our parents to be happy about us being together, so Derek and I could move forward, but it was starting to seem less and less likely that would ever happen. I could tell that their disapproval was taking a toll on him and I was starting to feel that if things didn't change, then maybe it would be better for Derek if we broke up.

By then, Derek had stopped sharing with me how he felt about his relationship with his family. Maybe he just didn't want to care anymore. But I felt it was getting to him in the worst way. It got to the point where Derek would break down in tears sometimes. I couldn't handle seeing him like that. I wanted him to be able to work through his issues and break away from his struggles, but instead I watched him crumble.

When we were out together, Derek would have to park around the corner from his house so his mom wouldn't see me. One day, I was waiting in his car and he came back crying, tears rolling down his face. I asked, "Derek why are you crying?" But I already knew the answer. I wanted to make a point, so I didn't pause and said, "You need to speak up for yourself. Maybe you should start saving up money to get your own place. Or maybe you could go live with your dad."

He turned away and said, "No, Farrah, you don't get it." He didn't want to hear my solutions to his problems. I tried to help him see that he needed to be stronger, but he just shut me out. I didn't know what to do. I wanted to help him, but he didn't want my advice. I felt guilty that it was because of me that he seemed to have even more problems than before, but what could I do if he wouldn't let me help him?

Watching the person you love suffer and being shut out when you want so desperately to help takes a toll. It was at that moment, sitting next to him in his car that day, that I started to go numb. All of a sudden, I needed to put up a barrier between us.

I wanted better for Derek. I loved him no matter what and would always be there to help him and hear him out. So when he shut me out, I felt hurt. I started thinking, *What am I really here for?* I felt that if he couldn't make the right choices to help himself then maybe I was the one who would have to make a choice. I needed to get away from his family and I hoped Derek would follow my lead.

The next day I called to see how he was doing and Derek told me that he had talked to his dad, and that his dad had invited him to come live with him in Missouri. Derek added, "He even said you could come live with us, too."

Derek's father lived three hours away in Missouri and they only saw each other every couple of months or so, but they were close. I hadn't met him yet, but, judging by how happy Derek was when he talked about his dad, I felt their relationship must be good.

I was happy for Derek, but I wasn't ready to move out of my house. I loved every inch of my bedroom, and, while things weren't great with my parents—mainly because of me dating Derek—I was trying to get along with them better.

There was just no way I could move to Missouri with him, so I told Derek that it was great that his dad had offered him a place to live and that I thought it was the right thing to do, but that I couldn't go with him.

I said we could still date long distance, but Derek didn't want to go alone. I think he was scared of leaving his life behind. He said, "Forget it. I'm not going to move away from my friends."

I realized I wasn't ever going to get through to him.

# OUR (FIRST) BREAK-UP

As the week went on, I kept distancing myself from Derek. I lost interest in hanging out with him after school, and when we had sex it seemed like we did it just to relieve our stress. I didn't even want him walking me to class anymore. Then something happened that made it clear to me things were not going to get better.

There was this guy whom Derek had started hanging out with more, though at the time I didn't realize it. He was part of our crowd and very popular, but he didn't hang out with us as much as he did with this group of jocks. Still, I knew this guy because he and I were always in the same lunch group. We hung out a lot at lunch and gossiped. One day, on the way to class after lunch, he said to me, "You know, Derek was out last night hitting on some girl."

He caught me off guard and I didn't know what to say.

Then I saw Derek standing in front of our locker and the sight of him filled me with rage. How dare he hit on another girl, after I had been so devoted to him and had tried so hard to help him deal with his problems. By the time I reached our locker, I was fuming. I looked at Derek and snapped, "I think maybe we shouldn't date anymore. You should probably go back to using your own locker and hitting on other girls."

Derek looked stunned. "Why? Why do you want to break up?"

"Well, I just heard that you were hitting on some girl last night."

Derek got so heated, I could tell he wasn't really listening anymore. "Who told you that?" he demanded

I glared at him and told him my source. "Apparently you were out with him last night and he saw you hitting on some girl."

Derek looked away. He said, "That's fucked up that he would say that. I'm going to go talk to him right now," and he immediately walked off to find his friend.

We didn't talk again until later that night. Derek called me and insisted his buddy was lying. I asked why he would make up something like that.

He said, "You know, he probably just wants to hook up with you."

I said, "Derek, he knows I'm not into him, so there's no reason for him to tell me that unless it was true."

His only response was, "I didn't do it."

He was quiet for a while and then he said, "I gotta go."

I wanted to believe him, but I couldn't let it go. The next day, during lunch I asked his friend again, "So, did Derek really hit on some girl?"

He looked at me pityingly. "That's what Derek is like, Farrah. Makes no difference to me if you don't want to believe me."

When he said he didn't care if I believed him or not, I could tell he meant it. He wasn't trying to create drama or hit on me. He was just telling me what he saw, as a friend. That's when I knew for sure that Derek was lying.

After lunch Derek came by the locker. I glared at him and said, "What are you doing here? We're done!"

He didn't respond, but the look on his face said, *What can I do to fix this?*

I spat, "If you really cared about me, you wouldn't be hitting on other girls. So we're done!"

"We're done because I hit on one girl?"

Suddenly, everything I had been holding in came out. "No, Derek, it's more than just that. It's the lies, it's how you treat me, and it's what you do when I'm not around. So don't come to my locker anymore. We're done."

And with that I walked away.

# WITHOUT THIS RING...

I continued to walk away from Derek—in the hall, in class, and at our locker. But Derek refused to accept that we were broken up. He kept trying to check in with me between classes by meeting me at my locker, or sending me text messages asking what I was doing after school.

After two weeks of being on Bad Boyfriend Probation, he was really starting to get desperate to talk to me and get me back in his life. Two days before Christmas break, he started writing me letters, and then one morning, out of the blue, in between classes, he handed me a note and a small box. I looked down at the box in my hand—it was a ring box. I looked up at Derek and he was smiling. I didn't know what to do. I spouted, "Uh, I need to hurry to class."

With my mouth probably still hanging open and my eyes wide from shock, I stuffed the letter and ring box into my purse and rushed off to computer class, I was trying to act like nothing had happened, but this was a big deal to me. I wanted to feel happy, but this was not how I had envisioned being given a promise ring. I had pictured it as a romantic moment and that we would be madly in love (or at least getting along), not as some desperate, hurried exchange in front of my locker in a crowded school hallway, when were broken up.

Still, I was dying to read Derek's note and look at the ring. I told myself that if Derek at least wrote a sweet letter, then I could overlook the otherwise total lack of romance. Maybe I could just look at it as an interesting story to tell our friends, or even our kids one day.

I finally got a chance to look in my bag when my teacher stepped out of the classroom for a few minutes. I dug the letter out of my bag and read it. Derek wrote that he loved me and that he and his dad had picked out the ring together. I thought that was so adorable. When I finally cracked the ring case open to take a peek, I almost shouted out, "Oh my God, this is the ring I wanted!" but I managed to contain myself. Smiling from ear to ear, I pushed the letter and ring back into my bag. I was so happy, thinking everything was sweet and great with Derek again. But…

In the pit of my stomach was a feeling of unease that I couldn't ignore. As class wound down, I started thinking of all our problems, of all Derek's issues that made our relationship such a struggle. What if, even with this ring, all the negative drama continued? What if Derek kept lying to me? What if I couldn't handle dealing with his family problems anymore?

By the time the bell rang and class was over, I was more confused than ever. At lunch I showed my friends the ring. They thought it was beautiful and couldn't understand why I felt like I shouldn't keep it. Of course, I wanted nothing more than to keep the ring, but there was no reason for me to have it if we weren't together and, if I couldn't trust Derek, how could we be together?

As much as I wanted the ring and as much as I wanted things with me and Derek to be perfect, I realized that I needed to slow down and think clearly before I got wrapped up in this promise ring and let it go to my head. After all, Derek's problems hadn't gone away, just because he had given me a ring. And the ring didn't alter the fact that he had lied to me.

My head was spinning. If Derek and I got back together, I wanted to start off on the right foot, but the way he had given me this ring, so rushed and unromantic and with us broken up, we were already very much on the wrong foot. It made me sad to think about giving back this perfect ring, but I really thought, *If I give this ring back now, he can give it back to me when were are happy, when there's no drama, and hopefully when we are out of high school.*

By the end of lunch, I had decided to give Derek back the ring and I wrote him a letter explaining why. I had also come up with a plan to get us back on track. I thought, *First, over Christmas break, I'll work on him so he knows how to treat me properly. Second, I'll spark a new and energized romance between us.*

Lunch ended and it was time to face Derek. I was sure that I would see him at my locker, so I grabbed my books and waited for him to come by. Finally, just as the bell was going to ring, I saw him walking towards my locker. When he got there, I grabbed my letter and the ring and quickly reached for his hand and shoved them in it before he even realized what was happening.

I said, "Here, take it and read my letter," and walked away.

I dreaded giving that letter to Derek because I knew it was going to hurt him. It was the hardest thing I ever had to do. I had written:

*Derek,*

*There is something in my heart that loves you so much. I have always loved you. It's just that I tried to think of honest good times with you, but instead all the bad times overtake the good. I will always be there for you as a friend. I can't date you anymore, at least not right now. I don't know how long this feeling will last. The ring you picked, I like it so much. It's perfect. But I can't keep it because it means nothing if we're not together. So I want to say thank you, but I can't accept it.*

*- Farrah*

After I stuffed the note in his hand, I didn't look back. I took off, like I was in a relay race and had just been passed a baton. I kept going even as I was regretting every step away from Derek I took. I just kept repeating to myself, *We're broken up. I'm too young for this. He flirted with ugly girls.*

As bad as it felt, I knew that giving him the ring back was the right thing to do. It was more than the lies. I was beginning to feel that Derek was mostly reacting to how unhappy he was. I had tried to help him. Tried to get him to see that he needed to get away from all the things in his life that seemed toxic to me, but he had made it clear that he wasn't going to do that. In a way I felt that Derek was letting me down and that made me sad. I couldn't go on taking all the abuse when he should have been directing his anger elsewhere.

After I gave him my letter, Derek wrote me back, saying that the ring was supposed to be my Christmas promise ring. What he wrote still haunts me. He pleaded for one more chance. He begged me to stay in his life. He thanked me for helping him get off drugs and promised not to let me down.

That night, we talked on the phone. As much as it broke my heart, I knew I needed to be strong and stand my ground. I said, "I think we really need this break. I'll call you over break if I want to hang out."

After my last class on the last day of school before Christmas break, I went to my locker to put my books away. I was happy I didn't have to look at those books for two whole weeks. I had been thinking about Derek all day and when I looked down at the bottom of my locker I saw that he had left another note for me. It said, "please call me" in all caps. He wrote that he really wanted to work this out, and signed the note "Cheese Nuts."

"Cheese Nuts" was a silly nickname I had made up for Derek and I loved when he said it back to me. I fell in love all over again and wanted to let my guard down. I loved Derek so much, but I didn't want to let him off easy. I needed him to work hard to get on my good side again.

Winter break started with a few texts from Derek here and there and a call to say "hi." He seemed bored. I could tell Derek was waiting for me to invite him to meet up with me and, secretly, I was missing him, too.

Christmas went by and we didn't talk. No "Merry Christmas." Nothing. I was determined to have a fun break, so I started hanging out a lot with my girlfriends. We went to parties and hung out with boys who liked us. I was back to being single again, but Derek was never far from my mind.

After a while, my girls and I got bored with those boys and I called Derek to invite him to go to a party with me and a friend. Since he said he'd gotten into trouble and had his car taken away again, we ended up picking him up. That night was an eye-opener for me. I began to really see for the first time that Derek was going down a path that I wanted no part of.

The party was at an older, college friend's house and at first Derek stayed by me on a couch in the corner, but then I got up to go to the bathroom and when I came back he was gone. I asked my friend if she had seen where he went, but she had no idea.

I started walking back towards the bathroom, when I saw a shadow in the hallway out of the corner of my eye. I looked closer and saw two bodies standing close together, and then I could make out that it was Derek with a girl.

I thought I saw her put something into his hand.

I wasn't sure what had just happened. I just knew that I wanted to get as far away from Derek as possible. I didn't know if they were trying to hook up or if she was slipping him pills. I didn't want to know. I just walked in the other direction and didn't stop until I found my friend. I said to her, "Let's go. We're leaving Derek. I just caught him with this girl back there and he's hiding something."

My friend was down with leaving and we were almost at the car when Derek walked out of the house and called out, "Wait! I'm coming with you."

I said, "No, you're not. You can just go be with your friend and keep hiding shit from me."

He yelled, "Nothing's going on!"

I just laughed, shut my door and waved. As we drove off, Derek shouted, "You're going to make me walk home in the snow?"

Later, I got a voicemail from him saying how fucked up I was for making him walk home in the snow. Maybe I was a bitch for leaving him, but he was a jerk and a liar for sneaking around and doing whatever he was doing behind my back. Clearly, my plan to teach him how to treat me properly and to rekindle our spark had completely backfired.

After a couple of days, I called him back. He was still mad at me, but he confessed that his sister had picked him up and driven him home. I knew he never would have had to walk home in the snow.

# REBOUND GUY

At this point, things between Derek and I were so bad that I felt like we really were never going to get back together. I couldn't talk to any of my friends about him because they knew how much he had hurt me and they wanted me to move on and date other guys.

So I went to a basketball game at another high school with a girlfriend who was dating a guy from that school. She wanted to introduce me to one of his friends. She said, "He's the most popular guy at this school. He's the best at basketball and he just broke up with his girlfriend." This was her way of trying to sell this guy to me.

I responded, "Well from watching him play basketball, he doesn't seem that great. I've never talked to anyone black before." This was true. My town is mostly white and I had led a pretty sheltered life.

She said, "He's not gangster. He's really nice," and with a wink she added, "and you know what they say about black guys!"

After the game, we waited in her car for the guys to come out. First my friend's boyfriend came over and then they called over the guy they wanted me to meet. He walked to my side of the car and introduced himself. He was tall, confident and cute. The only thing about him that fell short of my expectations was his car—it was kind of a beater. But then again I didn't even have a car, so who was I to judge?

He told my friend to give me his number and we started texting. Before I knew it, we were settling into a relaxed couple vibe. At first I allowed myself to be swept up in the ease of being in a relationship, but I couldn't get Derek off my mind. That's when I really learned the meaning of the word "rebound." Thank you, Rebound Guy!

So, Rebound Guy invited me over to his house and snuck me into his room. It was like I hadn't learned anything from getting caught sneaking around with Derek. I should have known sneaking into a boy's bedroom after curfew would lead to sex, but I thought if I had my guard up, it would be like a sleepover and nothing would happen. I just wanted to hang out with this new guy and show my friends that I was trying to get over Derek.

We were in his room downstairs, about to go to sleep, snuggling and talking. Truthfully, it was really awkward. I wasn't used to hanging out one-on-one with guys other than Derek. We really didn't have that much in common and it sort of felt like my friends had asked this guy to be my pick-me-up because I had been feeling so down about Derek.

I was trying to fall asleep and then all of a sudden we were making out and taking it all the way. It was good, but I felt like I had completely gone against my morals by having sex with someone I knew I was never going to be in love with. I was shocked by my behavior. I had never imagined having an experience like this with any guy other than Derek.

I didn't want anyone outside of my circle of friends to know that I had hooked up with Rebound Guy or to find out that we had slept together. Maybe I would tell Derek…eventually. There was a part of me, though, that was glad I had experienced sex with another guy. In a way, it made me feel like I could relate more to Derek, since he'd had sex with six other girls. I tried to be positive about it and see what would come out of this new experience.

Around this time, one of my friends had a pregnancy scare and a bunch of us decided to go to Planned Parenthood after school one day to get birth control. When I told Rebound Guy I had gone on the pill, I was surprised that he didn't seem more supportive. We had used a condom the time that we had sex and I planned to keep using them, to protect myself from STDs, but I felt like it would be a plus if I was on the pill. The only reaction I got from him was, "That's good for you."

I could tell he was trying to distance himself. I said I would talk to him later and told my girls about his less than enthusiastic reaction. I confided that I wasn't happy about having sex with someone I knew I didn't love and that I was still confused about where Derek and I stood.

Meanwhile, I honestly tried to get to know Rebound Guy. It took me weeks to sort things out in my head. I would go to his house after practice; we would talk, watch movies, go to parties and hang out with mutual friends. We were good together. We were popular; we had fun and other people were jealous of us being together. But we could sense that we each had unfinished business with our exes. We were both attached to what we had, and our exes were starting to act out behind our backs out of jealousy.

I was never blown away by Rebound Guy, but at least at first there was no drama. That didn't last long, though. Our relationship hit the breaking point after about a month. We went to a party together and the next day at school gossip about us caught up to Derek's sister. She came up to me in the hall and asked if I was dating a black guy. It felt like some kind of accusation. I said, "Yeah," and kept walking past her. I knew damn well she was going to run back to Derek and tattle.

I guess she must have told Derek right away, because by lunch he was on the phone yelling at me. (Since our class schedules didn't allow us to see each other anymore, we had to call each other to talk during school.) I let him yell for a while and then told him I would call him back.

I knew I had to break things off with Rebound Guy. That day I told him that Derek was mad we were talking. He said he understood because supposedly his ex-girlfriend was jealous, too. He confided that she tried to talk to him every day at school and that she was doing everything she could to get him back I was worried that she was going to talk trash about me or inch her way towards Derek, and that thought was intolerable. We agreed to quit hanging out together.

Once I had settled things with Rebound Guy, it was time to figure out where I stood with Derek. I didn't call him back when I said I would. Instead, I texted him and told him I needed to tell him something and I would call him later that day. After my last class, I went into the bathroom to call him. I desperately wanted to get back together with Derek and have everything work out and be fine. I wanted to forget all our issues and act like we had never broken up. I wanted to be done playing games. I wanted Derek to be real with me about his feelings and I wanted to share my honest feelings, too. I knew it was going to be hard, but I took a deep breath and called.

Derek was at home and it sounded like he was in his room.

I said, "Derek I'm going to tell you something and I don't want you to get mad. I'm going to be honest with you, okay?"

He agreed, "Okay, tell me."

"I did have sex with that guy. I don't know why I did it, but you should understand. You've had sex with more than one person. I've only had sex with you and that was hard to deal with."

Derek started yelling, "I loved you and you went and had sex with a nigger. I fucking hate black people."

I let him vent and get all of his anger out. He was devastated and crying Derek wasn't a racist. He had black friends and I had never heard him say anything racist before. I think he was just so angry at the thought that I had slept with another guy that he was lashing out and trying to say the most awful, hurtful thing he could think of. This sounds crazy, but it showed me how much he really cared about me.

It got quiet on the other end of the phone, and finally I spoke. I said, "I love you Derek. I needed to figure some things out. I'm telling you the truth because I care about you. I'll call you later and we can talk more."

I felt bad, but at least now Derek and I were being open about our feelings. We talked a little bit on the phone every day for the next week and it seemed like we were getting closer.

Unfortunately, we still had a rocky road ahead of us.

# NO MR. NICE GUY

March came and the weather started warming up again. It felt good. I was busy with soccer practice and there was a lot going on that time of year—grades, parties, getting ready for end-of-year stuff. Derek and I were still talking on the phone, but we weren't really seeing each other. I wasn't quite ready to get back together with him and I had no idea what he was really up to.

One afternoon at practice, I was in line to practice shooting goals when I overheard some girls talking. I could tell they purposely wanted me to overhear, so I acted like I was ignoring them and didn't give them the glory of bothering me. They were talking about how their friend had had sex with a boy at some party and they kept going on and on about it.

Then they asked me, "Didn't you date a Derek Underwood?"

I ignored them and focused on my ball.

Again they asked, "Hey, didn't you date a Derek Underwood?"

I turned around and said, "Yeah, a while ago. Who cares?"

I moved forward, kicked my ball and switched lines.

When I got out of practice, I called Derek. He picked up his phone and when he realized it was me he got all weird. He said he was in the shower and I thought, *Why would you pick your phone up in the shower?*

I was aggravated, but I heard the water running, so I just came out with it, "Did you hook up with with some girl at a party this past weekend?" Derek replied, "Yeah."

I said, "And you think that's okay?"

Derek said "Yeah. I have to go get ready. Bye."

I was disgusted and hurt. I thought, *Yeah, he has to shower to wash her off!* I couldn't believe that after everything Derek and I had talked about he would do this to me. Again! Now, every time I went to practice I would hear about Derek and this girl that was trying to be his girlfriend and the issues they were already having. It made me not want to go to practice anymore.

I knew I needed to quit breaking my dating rules and just move on. I was disappointed in myself, but I shook it off and decided this was my chance to get back on track. So I switched practice times and started dating a boy who had soccer practice with me. We had met at one of my part-time jobs the previous winter, so I had known him for a few months.

I figured he was the type of guy I should go for; he was nice, caring, and played sports. He really liked me. I met his parents and they liked me, which was a really nice change. We would go to parties and I would stay over at his place. He was so nice and cute and perfect, but I could not bring myself to kiss him or be anything more than friends. For a month and a half I seriously tried to make it work, but eventually I realized I was just using him to take my mind off of Derek.

I decided to be honest with him about how I felt, but he didn't take it very well. He couldn't let it go. He created tension and drama between my best friends and me, which made me feel that he wasn't such a nice guy after all.

I was so sick of the drama and I couldn't deal with stupid gossip anymore. I felt like I had something more important on my mind anyway, like, *How am I going to get Derek to come talk to me again and quit being a loser?*

Meanwhile, on top of fighting with my own girlfriends, I had to watch Derek and his new girlfriend holding hands walking down the hall. Derek would practically rub it in my face. I was going through mad hay fever and for days I looked like I had been crying my eyes out over him and his new sweetheart. My life was sucking wind.

I stopped talking to everyone who brought drama into my life. I only talked to my guy friends who had my back. They would come by my soccer practice and tell me what Derek had been up to. They told me he had started smoking. I was shocked because Derek had told me he would never smoke and didn't like it when other people did. I kept hearing negative rumors about Derek. I didn't want to believe any of it, but then one day my friend and I went to the Walgreens across the street from my school. I saw Derek walk in and I was going to go talk to him, but then I saw him walk out and the alarm went off.

He didn't stop at the register and the alarm had gone off, so I figured he must have stolen something. But I kept my mouth shut and didn't say anything to my friend who was with me. My friends didn't want to hear about Derek anymore anyway. I decided to just let it go. I realized that if he really didn't want to talk to me anymore, I needed to accept it.

But I couldn't help thinking, *What's happening to Derek?* He was smoking and now it looked like he was shoplifting? I felt like it was my fault. I broke up with him and gave his ring back. I had sex with some other boy and told him about it. I felt like I had pushed him over the edge and now I wasn't there for him when he was clearly self-destructing.

# DUDE, THERE'S A HAIR IN MY TACO!

Meanwhile, I had started talking to a preppy skater boy who I had kind of always had a crush on. I was sick of Derek and when you're sick of a boy sometimes the only answer is to talk to other boys. One day I went up to Skater Boy and said, "Let's go out tonight." I thought he had a girlfriend but he agreed to go out with me, so I figured they must have broken up.

That night, Skater Boy and I went to my college friend's party and I drank enough jungle juice to forget where the potty was. The next morning, my alarm went off at 5:00 AM and I found myself in Skater Boy's bed, spooning him. I untangled myself, stood up and whispered loudly while tapping him, "Hey, you need to get up. I have to go to work. Can I borrow some shorts? Mine are wet."

He got up and threw me some shorts. I ran to the bathroom and peed. The release felt good because my bladder was so full from all the alcohol I had drunk the night before. When I came out of the bathroom, Skater Boy told me to call him later and I went to work. So on my break, I called, like I used to do with Derek, but this call wasn't as cute.

When he picked up, I said, "Hey, I'm on a break. Figured I'd call you quick."

He answered, "Are you okay? Do you remember anything from last night?" He didn't seem concerned. I was getting more of a smartass vibe.

Right away he said, "Dude, you pissed all over me and my bed last night!!"

I started laughing, "Huh? I don't get it. I peed this morning after I got up."

Laughing, he said, "That's why you asked me for my shorts. Remember?"

I said, "Oh. You're probably right. Sorry about that."

"My mom had to wash my whole bed."

I was shocked and embarrassed, "Wow. You told your mom?"

He didn't answer that and skipped to the next subject, "My mom wants to invite you over for dinner tonight."

I was shocked. Seriously? After she cleaned up my pee? But I said, "Okay. I'll call you when I get off work."

After work I went home to change and Skater Boy came to pick me up. On the surface, he seemed to have everything I was looking for in a guy. He was a bit too much of a momma's boy for my tastes, but I did like that his parents were inviting me to dinner. After my experience with Derek's mom, I had learned how important it was to get along with the parents of the guy you're dating.

When we got to his house, I met his parents, who seemed really nice, and we played with his dogs. Then we sat down to eat.

A couple of bites in, I looked down and saw a huge hair trailing from my taco to my mouth. I tried to not to gag. I had to hide my disgust because his mom was in the middle of telling me something and out of the corner of my eye I could see Skater Boy looking over at me. Finally, I just reached down for my napkin and acted like I was wiping my mouth. I spit the food into my napkin and slowly put down the taco.

I looked down again. Now, there was a long taco hair dangling down from my face to my plate. It was totally noticeable, but no one said anything. I excused myself for the rest of the meal by saying I had an upset stomach. I actually really was feeling crampy, like I was about to get my period, so at least I was being honest.

After dinner, Skater Boy invited me to watch TV in his room.

He asked, "So how did you like my parents?"

I bluffed and said, "Oh they were nice and your mom cooked a good dinner."

I guess my answer made him feel pretty confident because the next thing I knew he was moving in towards my body. As we sat under his covers pretending to watch TV, he started rubbing my tummy and making his way down my pants. I wasn't really turned on and my cramps were getting worse, so I stopped him.

I turned the covers over and his bed was covered with blood. It looked like a massacre. Clearly my period had arrived. This was too much. I said, "Okay, maybe this is a sign that we shouldn't talk anymore. It's not working out." He seemed fine with that and took me home, but then called me later, saying he had told his ex-girlfriend about us. She was a good friend of Derek's sister, so I knew eventually it would get back to him.

The next day at school, I told my guy friends the whole story of what had happened with Skater Boy and they laughed. Then they told me that Derek had started working at Burger King. At least he had a better job when he was dating me. I thought, *Things just keep getting more and more depressing for Derek (and me) since we broke up.* He didn't even look the same anymore. He was skinnier and had blonde tips in his hair. It was hard for me to watch him changing like that.

# TIME TO TALK

On the days that I had PE and got out early, I noticed that Derek was always sitting in front of a classroom near my locker. We had stopped sharing a locker when we broke up, so he must have had a class nearby. I wouldn't even have to look, I just knew Derek was watching me as I waited at my locker for the bell to ring or as I walked to my locker in my gym clothes.

I liked it when boys would flirt with me right there in front of him. I was angry and wanted to make Derek feel like a loser for trying to make me jealous of him and his new girlfriend. After a couple of weeks of him watching me walk by, I started hearing rumors in the hallway that his girlfriend was mad at him. Supposedly, he wasn't picking up her phone calls or picking her up when he was supposed to.

It was actually hard to avoid hearing the gossip. It seemed like everyone around me was talking about them. I wondered if she wanted to get cooler by dating Derek. What she didn't realize was that Derek was looking totally uncool.

I felt like something was brewing and deliberately didn't put myself anywhere near her. I kept quiet and just observed the drama from a safe distance. It was entertaining, in a way, but I was disappointed that Derek wasn't smarter than this. The whole thing was pathetic.

Meanwhile, with only two months left in the school year, everyone was talking about graduation and prom. A guy friend had asked me to go with him to prom and I had said yes, though I couldn't help thinking about last year's perfect prom. Things were starting to look up for me, but I wondered how Derek was doing. I had no clue.

The next week, the storm I had felt brewing turned into a full-blown category five hurricane. I felt like his girlfriend was coming after me, talking about me in every class and yelling at me in the halls.

I assumed this meant that things between her and Derek weren't exactly going great, but I didn't want anything to do with it. I hadn't talked to Derek in what seemed like months. Then one day, he came over to my locker and said, "We need to talk." I walked away, but when I came back after class he was there again. I still didn't want to talk to him, though.

I went home and that night I thought about whether or not I should talk to Derek and give him another chance. I knew I should never take a guy back who stole, smoked, did drugs, and worked at Burger King, especially after he tried to make me jealous with some other girl. That all screamed, "Loser!" to me. But I still loved him and I couldn't help wanting things to work out between us.

The next day I finally agreed to talk to Derek. We left school to get away from his girlfriend, and went to a park to play basketball. While we were playing, we talked about what was on his mind. Basically, he said he wanted me to tell his girlfriend that he didn't like her anymore and that we were dating again. I felt bad for him, like I always did, even though I knew the situation he was in was his fault. It certainly wasn't my fault, but I told him, "Let's go back to school. I'll take care of it."

We went to see the assistant principal and I said, "Can I speak with you? I need your help." I went into his office, while Derek stayed in the waiting room. I told the assistant principal that Derek and I wanted to date again but that we were worried that his (soon-to-be-ex) girlfriend would cause trouble for us at school. The assistant principal looked at me like he thought I was out of my mind. He asked me if I was sure I wanted to get involved with Derek again.

I didn't know what to say. I had told myself that I would never break my dating rules and here I was embarrassing myself because I loved Derek, even though it felt like I didn't know him anymore.

Finally, I spoke up, "Yes. I'm serious. This girl he was dating won't leave me alone. I need her to quit talking about me, to quit trying to fight with me, and to leave Derek and me alone. We don't want her in our lives anymore."

The assistant principal agreed to help and called Derek's ex into the office. I could feel her anger as she walked by us. Derek and I sat together in the waiting room. I was sure she hated me. In the end, though, he must have gotten through to her, because from then on she left us alone.

After school, we went to the park by the river where we used to always hang out and I was happy that we could be friends again. I sat on Derek's lap, hugging him, squeezing his cheeks and giving him kisses. He said he wanted to start walking, so we walked along the dock. Some guys were looking at me and Derek noticed. He said, "Farrah, you know you're beautiful. I see guys looking at you all the time. You mean a lot to me and I really care about you." It felt good to hear that. It really made me feel like I had accomplished something, like he was finally starting to appreciate what he had.

He continued, "Let's go for a boat ride." We got on a little boat and I felt like we were that perfect couple again. I took pictures of us together with my cell phone. Looking back at those photos, I can see that Derek's skin was starting to look dull and muted. He wasn't the sexy, tan, healthy, muscular guy he had been when we first started dating. But, even at this low point, I can still see the happiness and love he had for me in his eyes and in his smile.

After our boat ride, I went home with just one thought running through my mind: *How am I going to get my parents to like Derek again?*

# PROM NIGHTMARE

So, Derek and I started talking again. I was low key about it with my friends, because no one wanted me to date him anymore. We would talk a lot at night and once a day at school. Slowly we started catching up. I told him I was now on birth control, but since I didn't really trust him yet, I insisted he get a STD test before we had sex again.

Eventually, Derek brought up prom. I told him that I had already agreed to go with a friend of mine. I felt bad because it was Derek's prom, his senior year, but no matter how much I would have preferred to go with Derek I had already committed to going with another guy and it wouldn't have been right to bail on him.

Derek let it go and just said, "Well I'm not going this year if I can't go with you."

I told him, "Ok, but I'm still going."

My date was into planning our prom night, getting our group together, setting up pictures, and getting a limo. Honestly, I wasn't that into going to this prom. Last year's prom with Derek had been epic. I felt like nothing could top that night, and I definitely was not going to have sex with this guy. I borrowed a blue dress from a friend and did my own hair. Prom Date took care of the rest.

He showed up at my house and met my mom. She took photos and then we left to meet up with our group. We sat in the limo, all squished together because our dresses were too damn big, and drove to the restaurant that they chose. All of a sudden, Prom Date had the urge to put me on the spot. He said, "Farrah, I just want to say you look amazing." He was sitting diagonally from me and leaned in for a kiss.

I let one kiss fly, but then he wanted to move over and sit by me and kiss me some more. I said, "No. I'm not kissing you. What are you doing?" I never thought Prom Date would try to pull that "because it's prom night" excuse on me. He was supposed to be my buddy. But that's what this situation was turning into and I wasn't having any of it.

After that, it seemed like Prom Date's cocky side started coming out. He couldn't let it go that I didn't want to kiss him. He started making a public display, which made it seem like I was being a bitch and being mean to him. Really, though, I felt like these girls and their dates could keep giving me dirty looks and think whatever they wanted about me. I wasn't being mean. I just wasn't going to kiss someone I'd never kissed before or let him even think he had a chance to have sex with me at the end of the night, just because it was prom night.

So I started texting Derek. Earlier, he had texted me, acting normal about the day. He hadn't even mentioned prom. I texted back how unhappy I was and Derek came up with the perfect plan to get me away from Prom Date and his friends. We texted all through dinner and he promised to whisk me away from the after-party at our friend's house, so I wouldn't have to spend a minute longer than absolutely necessary with these awful people.

I still tried to be decent to Prom Date. Since he insisted on buying me dinner, I offered to share a meal to save him money, but he didn't want to do that. He ordered the same entree as me and we both ended up with half our meal on our plates at the end of dinner. When the bill came, I knew I had been right to try to share. I felt that at this point, I was going to have to walk on eggshells until I got away from Prom Date and his friends.

Derek kept calling me and wanted to come get me, but I told him I would feel bad if I didn't at least make it to the dance. We arrived at the same convention center where prom had been hosted the year before. There were no nervous feelings in my belly like last year, though. I didn't even want to take photos with Prom Date and I just sat for most of the night. I looked at everyone in our group as a blur. I wished I was with Derek. I wanted to get away from this supposed guy friend who I felt had turned out to want more.

Prom was ending and we all got ready to drive out to the party at our friend's house. I asked for the address and texted it to Derek so he could meet me there and save me from this prom nightmare. When we finally got to the party, I had had enough of Prom Date projecting innocence, when what he deserved was a slap in the face. As I changed in the bathroom, I heard him out in the living room talking angrily about me.

As far as I was concerned there was no real reason for him to complain. So I walked out and said, "You're a scumbag. After the way you've treated me, I'm leaving. I'm not staying to hang out and I'm not having sex with you!" Prom Date was silent. His friends looked embarrassed for him.

I got my stuff and waited in the front yard for Derek. Five minutes later, he drove up. I rushed to his car. We were so happy to see each other. I told him all about Prom Date and my prom group and that was the end of that nightmare.

We drove downtown to this club I had never heard of. I got the feeling this was more of a gay club; some people were on drugs, most were drunk, only a handful were sober like me. We got through the bouncers and it was crowded inside. I could hear the thumping of deep base techno, my favorite kind of music to dance to. We went past the bar into the main dancing room. There were mirrors everywhere, on every wall, even on the ceiling. There were stripper poles on the stage, for anyone to dance on. It was a room full of movement.

Derek took me and put me against the wall of mirrors and started dirty dancing with me. It was so flattering, how he started building the passion between us. I switched positions with him and was flirting with him and turning him on. We were so wrapped up in each other, both of us felt like we were the only ones in the room. As we danced, we stared at our reflections in the mirrored ceiling and walls, lusting over each other's bodies.

Derek was into me like he had never been before. We kept dancing and dancing. It felt like we were all that mattered. We knew we were hot. It was a moment that I never wanted to end.

Sadly, the moment did end, with the DJ shouting something loudly through the club. Suddenly we were aware of fifty pairs of eyes staring at us. No one in the room was dancing but us. We just laughed and kissed each other, and he said, "Let's go over there and see what all this noise is about." We realized that they were starting a dance-off competition, but I would rather have just gone on watching our reflections. Two AM hit and I was sweaty, tired, and completely happy. We left the club and Derek took me home. We parted, saying, "love you" and "'night" to each other.

From then on, Derek would meet me every day after PE. He showed Prom Date that he had never had a chance with me. It was funny, Prom Date would practically cuss out loud when he saw us. It seemed like he hated seeing Derek and I together.

Now everyone knew to leave Derek and me alone because we were going to be together no matter what. It was the last few weeks of my junior year and Derek's senior year. I had all my class work done, but Derek was freaking out that he wasn't going to pass math. We both stayed after school to make sure he got all his work done. With my help, he got his grades up and passed all of his classes. I was so happy that he was going to graduate.

# GRADUATION GAS-AND-GO

At the beginning of May, Derek graduated. I went to watch the ceremony with one of my friends whose boyfriend was also graduating. I was so proud of Derek for pulling it together and making it to graduation. I couldn't wait to see him looking all handsome in his cap and gown, but as I scanned the faces of the three hundred graduating seniors, I didn't see his. It was so crowded in the auditorium, I was starting to get anxious that I wouldn't be able to find him when it was over.

We listened to all the speeches and at the end of the ceremony I finally spotted Derek as he and his class threw up their caps to celebrate. I was so thrilled I jumped up and ran through all the people to reach him, but then I lost him again in the crowd.

I finally found him outside of the entrance doors, looking for me. He'd been digging through the crowds to find me, too. After we hugged, we went to find his dad. This was the first time I was going to meet his father and I was really looking forward to it. I'd heard so much about him and I already felt like we were going to get along.

I was also curious about his father because I figured he would be a living example of what Derek might look like when he was older. I was nervous and wanted him to like me. I felt like Derek's mom and I never hit it off, so this was my opportunity to make a good impression on someone in his family.

Derek and I held hands as we skimmed through the crowds of celebrating graduates and their families to find his dad. When we finally found him, they hugged and I introduced myself. His dad, Jerry, certainly wasn't the spitting image of Derek, but I saw big similarities between them. He was tall like Derek, with the same eyes, and they had similar personalities. It was great to finally meet him.

Jerry wanted to take us to lunch, so we went with some of Derek's closest friends to a restaurant nearby. I sat by his dad because I really wanted to get to know him and show him how much I cared about Derek.

While the guys were eating and talking, Jerry invited me to visit him in Missouri with Derek. The invitation made me feel so welcomed and I started to relax and feel confident that he liked me. I imagined how much fun Derek and I could have going down there together.

At lunch, Derek was so relaxed and happy. I could tell it meant a lot to him that his dad had come to his graduation and had taken me and his friends out. I hadn't see his mom (or his sisters) at the ceremony, but she was having a family gathering at her house for Derek later that afternoon.

So after the lunch with Jerry, we went to his mom's house. It was a very small gathering—only a couple of Derek's friends came. After a while I sensed something was wrong. We were all outside in the yard and I realized that Derek had disappeared.

I looked over at his mom, who was behaving like everything was fine. But I had a bad feeling, so I decided to go inside to look for Derek. I thought she might stop me from going inside, but she didn't.

I went downstairs to Derek's room and found him lying on his bed in the dark, his face to the wall, crying.

"Why are you crying? What's going on?" I asked.

"My mom promised to give me money for graduation and now she's not going to," he paused and then continued, "Because the police came to the house before we got here. I have to go to jail. My mom is having them come back tonight after the party."

"Why would the cops come for you, Derek?"

He looked sheepish. "I did a gas-and-go."

"What?"

I couldn't believe it. Not only was what he had done wrong and illegal, it was stupid. He should have known that if you fill your car up with gas and drive off without paying, eventually the cops are going to catch up with you. A security camera at the gas station must have caught his license plate number and the police were able to track him down at his mom's house. I was shocked and disappointed. I was also angry that I had to find out this way.

When Derek heard his mom come inside, he went upstairs to talk to her. I followed him up and watched as he tried to confront her about the money she had promised him. With me by his side, he felt more confident about approaching her.

His mom just ignored him. I completely disagreed with how she was handling things, but it wasn't my place to say anything. I just stood there staring as she walked away.

I was completely frustrated by the situation. On the one hand, I felt sad for Derek that his mom wasn't giving him the money she had promised him. But on the other, I was angry with him for breaking the law. I told Derek that what he'd done was stupid, but I also felt like if he had been strong enough to make the right choices on his own, he wouldn't have been in this situation in the first place.

Derek and I decided he should take me home and then go back home and deal with what he had done. He dropped me off (which I made him do around the block so my parents wouldn't see his car) and he was driving home, I called his cell. We talked until he got back to his mom's. I tried to help him think of ways to keep from having to go to jail. I suggested he go to the gas station and offer to pay the money. Maybe they would drop the charges.

I could tell Derek was listening, but he was very quiet the whole time. Then he said he was home and had to get off the phone because he had to go talk to his mom. I thought for sure I wouldn't hear back from him for the rest of the day and it was scary to be in the dark about what was going to happen to him.

I sat in my room, looking out the window and worrying about Derek. It was a beautiful sunny day and I could see my parents outside gardening. They still had no idea I had been seeing Derek again and this certainly wasn't the moment to tell them about it. A little while later my phone rang and it was Derek. I was surprised he was calling back so soon, but he kept it short.

"Hey babe. So my mom called the police to come get me from the house. They're going to be here soon."

"I hope you can just tell them you're going to pay them, and then you can get out of going to jail." I didn't know what else to say.

" I don't know…"

He was quiet again and I wondered what was going through his mind. I pictured him in his room. I could see it perfectly in my head; all the things written on his wall, my number, my friends' numbers, our prom photo, and other snapshots and mementos he'd put up on his wall. Lately, it seemed more obsessive—he had more photos of us in his room, more numbers on his wall.

It seemed like he was spending a lot of time in his room lately, and I didn't know what he was up to—and now this gas-and-go. In some ways Derek felt like a stranger to me these days. This wasn't the Derek I had fallen in love with.

"Babe, the police are here. I have to go. I'll call you when I get out."

I said, "Okay, I love you," and we hung up.

The next morning he called me as though nothing much had happened. He just said he'd had to pay a fine and changed the subject, asking me what I had done the night before. I knew he was still upset about everything, so I decided to let it drop. I was just happy he was out of trouble.

# LIAR, LIAR

Though Derek and the rest of the seniors were graduated and gone, I was still stuck in school 'til the end of May. I would usually ask Derek to come pick me up after classes let out. At first, he was good about being on time. I was starting to feel like, after his brush with jail, that maybe he was maturing and letting go of the bad habits he had fallen into during our break-up, but it wasn't long before I realized I was mistaken.

One afternoon, two weeks after graduation, I called Derek as soon as school got out, and when he answered he said, "I'm going to be late. I'll call you in ten." I hung up and waited for him. All my friends saw me waiting but I acted like everything was fine. I could tell by the looks on their faces what my guy friends were thinking: *She's letting Derek walk all over her again.* It was like they felt sorry for me, but didn't want to say anything to crush me more than I already was.

I waited and waited. An hour went by. Everyone else was gone. Finally, I called him again.

Me: "Derek where are you? You never called me back."

Him: "My mom came home and needed help. She's getting a dishwasher."

Me: "Okay, so when can you come get me?"

Him: "I don't know."

Me: "Okay. But I'm waiting on you. You were supposed to come get me."

Him: "Can't you call your dad?"

Me: "No. I'm waiting for *you*. You already said you'd come get me. Just hurry up, please."

Another five minutes went by, then ten. I kept checking my phone. No missed calls. Finally, fifteen minutes later, I saw his car. He showed up like he had nothing to explain to me. He was totally silent. I knew he had been lying to me about where he'd been, though. Derek always got quiet when he was lying to me. First of all, his mom was never home before school let out. She would have been at work. Second, the next time I came over, there was no dishwasher in the kitchen.

After that I started keeping count of every time Derek lied to me. I don't know why, because I never confronted him or did anything about it. But I realized Derek hadn't changed after all. He had just started living a double life. He was one person with me and another when he was with his buddies. He kept things hidden from me so I wouldn't call him on his bad habits and force him to change. But I saw signs of what he was really up to all the time.

The next day he told me he had to meet up with a friend for something, he didn't say what. I went along with him. We met him at a gas station and Derek gave him whatever they had met up for. Then his friend called through the window, asking Derek if he wanted to come smoke a bong. I looked at Derek, wide-eyed. He rolled his eyes at his friend and rolled up the window. He didn't say anything, just held my hand.

I hated feeling like when he was with me he acted like he would never smoke weed or do drugs, but then when I wasn't around he would allow himself to be pressured into making bad choices. I could always tell when he had been smoking weed before coming to see me. There were so many tip-offs: he'd have glazed eyes that he'd doused with eye drops, or he'd be chewing gum to hide the smell of his breath, or he'd stink like his sister's girly shower gel, or have sprayed on a shit ton of cologne to mask the smell. You can't really hide something like that from someone who sees you daily, and who used to do all of that stuff with you.

Derek could sense that I was mad at him and that I was getting suspicious, so he tried to make it up to me. A couple of weeks later, he told me he got a new job at a restaurant down by the boatyard. I knew exactly which place he was talking about. It was an upscale restaurant on the riverfront, and I was very happy for him because it seemed like a great job.

He said he wanted me to work with him, so we could be together more. He got me an interview with the manager after school one day and pretty soon I was working there too. I was happy about the job, but what really made me feel good was that I hoped if Derek and I spent more time together he would change back into the Derek I had fallen in love with.

# LATE

By the end of May school was out and summer vacation had finally begun. It was time for cheerleading camp, which was always the first week of June. I packed up my cheer camp clothes, plus extra socks, a bikini, and tampons. My period should have already come, but I figured it was running late.

Derek and I hung out one last time the night before I left and we promised to call each other every evening while I was at camp.

The bus ride to camp was tedious, but when we got to the University of Lincoln's campus I felt like I had arrived at home. That was me, I couldn't wait to go to college. Every year when we went to a college campus for cheer camp, it was the best—dorms, workout gyms, older college guys and pretty cheerleading coaches to look up to, eating camp food, sweating daily, getting sore muscles, building new ones, and having cheerleading chants engraved in my brain.

Ahhhh! I breathed it all in.

On the third day of camp, I felt like I was finally about to start my period, which was a relief because I was beginning to get worried. During lunch break, I went to the bathroom and peed, but when I checked the toilet the water only had pee in it—no blood. Then I looked at my underwear and there was one tiny drop of blood. I thought, *What does this mean?*

That night I told Derek that my period hadn't come and I was worried. Derek, as always, thought there was nothing to worry about. He said, "Sometimes girls don't get periods every month." I wanted to ease my stress, so of course I agreed, but all that week I worried. One drop of blood wasn't a period, but what was it?

# BRAWL AT THE SALTY DOG

At the end of that week I came home from cheer camp and it was back to work and tanning for the rest of summer. Working with Derek had been going well. We would eat together on our breaks or after we got off our shifts. We were spending a lot of time together just like he'd promised. But then one night at the end of June things changed.

My sister wanted to go out for her 21st birthday and one of her guy friends had rented a party bus. I told Derek I wanted to hang out with him later that night, but that first I was going to go out with my sister and my other friends for a little bit. I said I'd call him later.

As the night wore on, Derek got more and more annoyed with waiting for me. On top of that, he had gotten it into his head that a friend of my sister's liked me and had taken me on a couple of dates while Derek and I were broken up. It was true that the guy liked me and I had gone out with him a couple of times, but he knew how I felt about Derek and had never tried to hit on me. It was more like a friend who had a crush on me but was happy to just hang out.

It got to the point in our text messages where Derek was trash talking, saying he would fight the guy if I didn't tell him where I was and if I didn't let him come get me right away. I refused because he seemed so angry, but told him he could come get me later. By 1:00 AM our group had made its way back to our neighborhood to a bar called the Salty Dog.

I wanted to wait for Derek, so I didn't go inside. I told my sister how Derek had been acting, so she would know what was going on. I said that I thought it was best if I left before Derek got too jealous. She didn't like Derek because, like my friends, she had watched me get hurt over and over again. She was sick of the drama and didn't want to hear about it or deal with it anymore.

I told her I was going to text Derek and ask him to come pick me up. I stayed on the party bus and waited for him while everyone else went inside. I waited a good fifteen minutes on the bus with no sign of Derek. By now, I was tired of talking to the bus driver and feeling like I was being punished for my boyfriend's insecurities, so I thought, *I'll just go into the bar for a little bit and I'll keep watching for Derek. My sister will let me know when he's here.*

I went into the bar and, after another half hour, I figured Derek wasn't going to show up. I hadn't gotten any texts or phone calls from him and I didn't know where he was. I hung out and talked to friends and after a while I noticed that half of our group wasn't in the bar anymore. I figured they were all outside talking or smoking, but then I noticed that my sister was upset about something and had got up and left the bar. So I went to see what was going on.

I walked out the door of the bar and in the parking lot I saw Derek and a friend of his were fighting with my sister's friend. They were all hitting each other, and I saw my sister run over and hit Derek too. I was freaking out. I felt like I should protect Derek, but those were my friends and my sister he was fighting with.

Just then Derek looked up and saw me. That seemed to enrage him even more, and he started yelling at all my friends. He didn't say one word to me, though. I didn't know what to do, so I ran away from it all to my sister's car. Two minutes later the cops showed up and everyone scattered. My sister and her boyfriend met me at the car and I asked, "Why were you fighting with Derek?"

She was pissed. "He came here wanting to fight and talk shit, so he's going to get hit."

As we drove off I looked out the car window. I looked for Derek but his car was gone. After how he had ignored me, I figured we were done.

# COLD WAR GAMES

The next day I went to work, but Derek wasn't there. It was a Sunday, so it was pretty quiet and I had a good shift with great customers. I focused on work and tried not to think about the night before. Finally, when things were winding down, my manager came over and said he wanted to talk to me.

"So, Farrah, what happened last night?"

"What do you mean?" I asked.

He looked at me strangely. "Derek called in to say he couldn't work his shift because he had to go to the hospital last night. He fractured his wrist and hurt his arm. He said he got into a fight because of you."

I was pissed because I felt like Derek was trying to get back at me for the fight by getting me fired.

"It wasn't my fault. I was waiting for him to pick me up, and *he* started the fight with my friend. When I left the bar, his arm and everything seemed fine. As far as I know, he didn't break anything last night. My sister told me all they did was hit him on the head."

"You know, Farrah, sometimes guys might keep a girl around because it's comfortable, but maybe you should move on."

I knew he was trying to help and give me advice, but hearing that really hurt, though I tried not to show it. I didn't want to accept what he was trying to tell me. I told myself that Derek only keeping me around because it was comfortable made no sense. His friends didn't like me and my friends and family didn't even want us talking to one another. That's not comfortable.

Still, I replied, "I'll think about it."

Derek didn't text or call me, so once again I had no idea what was going on in his life. When I didn't hear from him by the following Friday I was sure we were done. That night, I got to work early. I said "hi" to everyone and made a special effort to be nice to Derek's guy friends, hoping I could get them to spill to me what he had been up to, even if they were on Derek's side.

Derek hadn't shown up to work yet, though it was past the time he was supposed to be there, and I overheard one of his guy friends saying, "Derek better show up and not let Farrah win."

I thought, *What game are we playing? I haven't even talked to him.* But when Derek showed up I caught on to what game he wanted to play. He walked in and all the guys high-fived him and cheered. I played it cool and acted like I didn't notice. A mutual friend filled me in later about what was going on in the restaurant, because I was up front hosting.

He said, "Derek is back there, talking about some girl and how she picked out the color for his cast. He's talking likes she's his new girlfriend."

I acted like it didn't bother me. "That's cool. I don't really care. Good for him, 'cause my friend hit him in his face."

The night wore on and we all focused on doing our jobs—hosting, running food, serving. I overheard Derek a couple of times talking loudly about some girl and then looking at me as I walked up to the host stand.

Our mutual friend came over again. "Farrah, I think he's making some of this stuff up. We're not asking questions, but he keeps talking. He just wants to get you mad, girl."

Again I just said, "I don't care."

Everyone was looking for me to react to Derek's games, but I wasn't going to let him get the upper hand. I did my hourly cleaning and then took my break. I got ice cream for dessert and the girls wanted pickles so I got some pickles, too.

I was almost done eating when one of the servers noticed me. "Girl, you're eating ice-cream and pickles. You know what that means," and he laughed.

I said, "No, what does it mean?"

He looked surprised, "It means you're pregnant."

"I don't think so." I was so angry at Derek and distracted by his games that I couldn't think straight. Then another host at the stand, said, "I could never picture Farrah pregnant. It's not possible. She's so tiny, a baby would never fit."

I said, "Yeah, I have a six pack."

I laughed, but it did worry me. I still hadn't gotten my period since before cheer camp and because of everything being so up and down with Derek and me, we hadn't gone yet to get me a pregnancy test. I realized I would probably have to deal with it on my own, but I pushed it out of my mind.

The following week at work another mutual friend mentioned that she had helped Derek with a tire issue the other night. She said his whole tire flew off his car. I laughed because I used to tell him all the time to fix that tire, but I didn't want to think about Derek. I wondered why she was talking to me about him. She knew we were fighting and I didn't need to hear that they were hanging out.

Finally, I said, "Why are you talking to me about Derek? I don't care if you're friends, but I don't want to talk about him."

"Well, I just don't want you to get mad at me. We're friends and he gets me weed." I was silent for a moment. I couldn't believe Derek was dealing weed at work.

"I don't care. I just don't want to hear about it."

For the rest of the day, it felt like Derek was trying to test me. He kept asking my friend to go smoke with him—it got really irritating.

Eventually, our manager came up and asked where she was.

I said, "I think she went to smoke."

Our manager looked annoyed. "How many times has she gone out already? And how long has she been out there this time?"

I said, "I don't know. Maybe five minutes."

I was lying, but I didn't want to get her in trouble, especially when it was really Derek's fault.

My friend came back in and said, "The manager's mad at me. She said I can't smoke anymore."

"Sorry. I tried to stall, but we needed more help."

The next day when I got to work, Derek was flirting with one of the other employees. At first I was hurt, but then I remembered how, when she started working there, Derek had said, "She's kind of ugly and looks like a nerd. I wonder why they hired her," and I realized this was just another one of his games to make me jealous.

That whole shift, Derek kept walking around me like I didn't exist, and he kept coming up to the host stand flirting with the other hostesses. All the girls began talking about him flirting with them. I knew his flirting was an act, but the girls sure thought he was being sincere.

Finally, I said, "Derek is so annoying. He's just trying to make me mad!" A lot of the girls who had known that Derek and me were dating agreed. One said, "We don't get why you ever dated him. He looks gay." But the newer girls acted like he really wanted to date them.

I worked late that night. After I finished cleaning the bathroom at the end of my shift, I was starving, so I decided to eat at work. I got my food and sat down. I was winding down from working all day, listening to the music from the outside bar, when suddenly Derek came over and sat down opposite me. I was surprised because I thought he had already left for the night.

I said, "Hi," and looked down at my food. Out of the corner of my eye, I could see our managers staring at us, probably just as confused as I was.

Derek said, "We need to quit fighting and work through our problems."

I was caught off guard. I had been feeling so anti-Derek and he had been ignoring me, so where was this coming from?

I said, "I'm not fighting."

I wanted to act like I didn't care but then the irritation I had been holding back got the better of me and I blurted, "But I guess you're hanging with some other girl now, since she picked out the color of your cast for you, and you've been hitting on all the hosts and giving weed to people at work."

Derek looked surprised. "I'm not hanging out with any other girl. I'm friends with other girls, just like you're friends with other guys, and it's someone else who's selling weed to people. Not me. I'm just his friend."

"So that makes everything better? Sorry, I'm not talking to you anymore."

Derek sat there quietly and I finished eating. When I was almost done, he leaned forward and said, "Can I take you home?"

"Yes."

That's all it took.

I was quiet in the car and just said, "bye," when we got to my house. I wasn't sure what was going to happen in the future, but I was happy we were at least talking again.

After that, I decided it was best to let our co-workers go on thinking that we were still fighting. Derek wasn't too happy about it, but I was sick of everyone knowing my business. People would make comments like, "Derek looks like a sad puppy dog today." Or they would ask me, "When are you two going to get back together again?" but I didn't answer. I wasn't sure how I felt about us talking again and it was easier to keep it private.

One night after work, we went to the riverfront and walked for about ten or fifteen minutes. Derek tried to hold my hand the whole time, but I wouldn't let him. He was really trying to connect with me, but I didn't want to get hurt anymore. I could tell he was upset that I wasn't being nicer to him.

He said, "You act like you don't care about me anymore."

"Derek, I do care about you, but we're better off as friends right now."

He stopped walking and turned to face me. "My uncle died today and you don't even care!"

Instantly, I stopped being mad. All my love for Derek just welled up inside me. I hugged him and asked, "How did he die?"

"I don't want to talk about it. My mom just found out today."

"I'm really sorry. I know how much you loved your uncle."

I looked at Derek. He was crying. I remembered meeting his uncle and how nice he had been to me. He had been one of the few people in Derek's family who seemed supportive of our relationship. I knew Derek looked up to his uncle and remembered how impressed he had been with his uncle's burnt orange Mitsubishi.

"Yeah. I'm going to miss him a lot." Derek grabbed my hand. "Farrah, let's start talking again. We can take things slow."

It hurt me to see Derek so upset and I wanted to make him happy again. I couldn't say no. I loved him too much. So I hugged him and said, "Okay. I love you Derek."

# TIME TO FACE THE TRUTH

—··◁∞▷··—

The next week at work we started talking to each other in front of other people. The hostesses rolled their eyes at us and the guys were annoyed I was back with Derek. Our managers just seemed relieved we weren't fighting anymore.

Derek would take me home after work and one afternoon I talked him into letting me dye his hair—I couldn't stand those blonde tips anymore. We did it at a friend's house because my parents still didn't know we were together. Things had been so up and down since May that I had never found the right moment to tell them.

Derek's hair turned out a handsome brown color. His tips were gone and he looked like his old self. It was like we were officially best friends again. I would sneak Derek into my house occasionally and we would go out together. Everyone at work told us we now looked like brother and sister because our hair color matched.

One day Derek met me at the restaurant before my shift. I was hungry, so I ordered some food from the bartender. He seemed to have a little crush on me, but I thought Derek would be cool with it because he wasn't as hot as Derek, so Derek had nothing to worry about. But after I ordered, Derek started getting huffy about the bartender flirting with me.

I said, "Let's eat outside," so we could get away from the situation before Derek made a scene. Derek followed me, but spouted out to the bartender, "Ugly mutherfucker!" on his way out. I kept walking and pretended I didn't hear. I thought it was mean of Derek to do that and I was embarrassed.

We sat down outside with our food and Derek seemed to be calming down. It was so nice and quiet by the water. There was a cool breeze and the sun was shining. The bartender brought my food out and set it down in front of me, emphasizing everything he did, being extra nice to get under Derek's skin. After he left, Derek got upset.

"You're not talking to him anymore!"

"I can talk to him if I want. I'm okay with him."

"Why would you talk to him? He shouldn't hit on you if we're talking. He doesn't respect that, so fuck him."

"Well, I'm going to talk to him because I have to work with him."

This discussion was going nowhere. I picked up my sandwich to take a bite, trying to inhale the taste and enjoy the view. Then the next thing I knew, Derek took my dish and flipped it over. Some of the food got on me and the rest went all over the floor. By the time I had swallowed my bite and could even say anything, Derek had stormed off and left me there. I was angry and humiliated, but I cleaned up the mess and acted like nothing had happened. I went inside to work and the bartender barely looked at me anymore.

The next day I told Derek that I needed to get a new phone. In the car on the way there we talked about getting a shared plan. Of course, I knew this was a big deal, but I felt like we needed something to show that we were committed.

We looked at phones and picked some out, but when we left the store only I had a new phone and contract. At the last minute Derek changed his mind. He didn't give me a reason. He just said that the phone he had was good enough for the time being. Since we were on our way to hang out at the pool, I let it go because I just wanted to relax and have a nice day with him. I wanted to feel like everything was perfect.

After we changed, we met by the pool and found chairs to lie on. We sat for about ten minutes, taking pictures and enjoying one another. Finally, the tension was gone and we were back to being a happy couple.

Then Derek's friend Bentley called. Derek was pretty quiet when he answered, so I wasn't sure what he was saying. But he got off the phone and ten minutes later, sure enough, Bentley popped up at the pool.

I was annoyed. I felt like we hadn't talked about inviting his friend to join us, so why was Bentley here? Plus, now Derek was talking to Bentley and ignoring me. I finally got so annoyed at being left out that I said something.

"Derek, why didn't you tell me your friend was coming? I thought this was our day to hang out alone together."

Derek didn't answer me. Then Bentley got mad because he thought I was being rude and he got up and left.

I said loudly, "How dramatic!"

Derek was pissed. "You don't need to be a bitch to my friends."

"Well, you don't need to be with Bentley all the time!"

Derek's phone went off again. I knew that it was Bentley, probably bitching about me, because Derek got off the phone, grabbed his stuff, and just left me at the pool. He didn't even say anything.

I was lucky I had my sunglasses on, so nobody noticed me crying. I sat there for ten minutes trying to calm down and figure out whom to call to come pick me up. I realized I had left my new phone and all my contract information in Derek's car, but fortunately I still had my old phone and hadn't turned off the service. I couldn't call my parents. This was definitely not how

I wanted them to find out I had been seeing Derek. I ended up calling my sister. She wanted to know why I needed a ride home from the pool, so I had to tell her, "Because Derek left me here."

While I was waiting for my sister to come get me, Derek called. I picked up and just yelled at him—about leaving me and about what an asshole he was. I pretty much didn't let him say anything. Then I hung up on him.

I waited in front of the pool 'til my sister picked me up. Then I had to admit to her that I had left my new phone in Derek's car. My sister wasn't happy about all the running around I was asking her to do for me, but she was even more annoyed by Derek and his behavior.

I was beyond mad. I was ready to hate Derek for everything and never speak to him again. But I had to get back my new phone, so I had no choice but to call him. He told us to meet him at his house, but when we pulled up, he wasn't even there. I tried calling and texting him, but he didn't pick up or reply to my texts. Finally, he pulled up around the corner and his dumb friend Bentley was in the car with him.

My sister was pissed. She glared at Derek. "You know, stealing phones, we could call the police for that."

Derek threw the phone over to her and then looked at me and said, "Love you, Babe!" and drove off.

I didn't know what to make of that. Was Derek being sincere or was he mocking me and throwing my love in my face? I was upset, but my sister didn't want to talk about what had happened. She was sick of Derek.

When I got home, I had to face the truth. I couldn't stand who Derek had become. I knew I couldn't hang out with him anymore. I went into work and switched my hours, so I would only work mornings and I wouldn't have to see him anymore.

# UNPLANNED PARENTHOOD

By now it was late July. A lot had happened since the end of June, and none of it made me feel like there was hope for Derek and me. I tried to keep busy, so I wouldn't dwell on how much he had hurt me over the past couple of months. I went to summer cheer practice and to work. When I wasn't doing that, I hung out and tanned with my friends.

But there was something else I had been trying to avoid thinking about, something that at this point I had no choice but to deal with: I still hadn't gotten my period.

I finally had to face the fact that something was really wrong. I wasn't just late. Now, when I did my abdominal planks during cheer practice, it didn't look like I had a six-pack anymore. It looked like I had a small triangle poking out of my tummy. I knew that I was probably pregnant and I started freaking out.

I confided in one of my closest cheer friends, Zabby. She promised she would keep it a secret and said I should get a test to make sure. But I didn't want to go with her to get the test because, even though we were close, you can't trust cheerleaders not to gossip. I couldn't ask Derek because he wasn't returning my calls, so I asked my girlfriend, Sadie, from work to go with me.

One day at work, I said to her, "Will you come with me to get a test to see if I'm pregnant?"

Sadie looked shocked. "Are you serious?"

"Yeah. I'm late, and my body feels different. My pants are tighter. I don't trust anyone else. Please?"

"Okay. I'll borrow my mom's car and come get you after cheer practice tomorrow." She knew all about my history with Derek and was really supportive.

After cheer practice the next day, Sadie picked me up and we went to the Planned Parenthood clinic, which is where I had gotten my birth control. Sadie came in with me and we sat in the waiting room until my name was called. I was so nervous, the wait felt like forever. When I finally heard the nurse call my name, I wanted to hide my face.

Sadie said, "I'll wait out here."

I got up and said, as cheerfully as I could, "Okay, see you soon."

As I followed the nurse, I had a million thoughts running through my head: *It's just nerves. It's the birth control making you fat*—anything that could possibly explain why I had put on weight other then the fact that I might be pregnant.

But now it was truth time. I would find out if I was or I wasn't.

The nurse led me to a restroom and told me to pee in the cup she gave me and then leave it in the restroom and come out when I was done. I peed into the cup and looked at it. It didn't look any different to me. It looked like my regular pee. *I don't think I'm pregnant*, I thought to myself. I set the cup on the sink and walked out of the restroom.

Then the nurse led me to an exam room and told me to wait there until she came back with the results of the test. I sat there and waited. I thought, *If*

*I'm not pregnant, I'm never having sex with Derek again, after all the shit he's done to me and now he's not even here with me. I'm going to quit having sex altogether.* Then I tried to think what would happen if I was pregnant, but my mind didn't want to go there.

After ten minutes, the nurse came in. I tried to be happy and cheerful, hoping that if I acted normal, everything would be fine and the test would be negative. I looked at the nurse's face. She didn't look happy.

"So, the test came back saying you're pregnant."

I went from cheerful and happy to hysterical and crying in one second flat. I was in a total panic and wanted someone to blame.

"If I'm pregnant, then it's your fault! I got my birth control here, so if it didn't work it's your fault I'm pregnant!"

The nurse tried to soothe me. "Honey, you need to calm down. Let's talk and figure this out. Have you been taking your birth control daily around the same time?"

"Yes, I make sure I do." I took my birth control pills religiously.

"Well, do you take any medications?"

I thought for a minute. "No I don't, but I did have to take a prescription antibiotic for my tonsils a while ago. My doctor thought I might be coming down with an infection."

"Well, based on the date of your last period, you could be as many as six weeks pregnant. Did you take the antibiotic four to six weeks ago?"

"Yes."

I felt like I couldn't sit in this room a second longer. I couldn't remember anyone explaining to me that medications could make my birth control pill ineffective.

The nurse looked at me sympathetically. She explained that it wasn't too late to terminate the pregnancy if that was what I wanted. I could either have a surgical abortion at a health center, or I could choose a nonsurgical method, called a medication abortion, which is an abortion induced with medications.

I asked her about the medication abortion and she explained, "There are two steps; first a medication is given in pill form at a health center, followed by a second self-administered medication taken at home. The first medication blocks the hormone progesterone, which causes the lining of the uterus to break down and prevents the pregnancy from continuing, and the second medication causes cramping and bleeding which expels the pregnancy."

She said that if I wanted to end the pregnancy, I could take this medication but that, since I was under eighteen, a parent would have to come in first and sign a form. This is not the case in all states, but in Iowa the law required the clinic to notify a parent. She told me to calm down and to go home and talk to my parents.

"I'll give you some time to yourself and you can come out when you're ready."

"Thank you," I said quietly.

I was sad, but I knew what I had to do now that I had found out for sure I was pregnant. I needed to call Derek. I got out my phone and dialed his number, but his phone rang and rang and then went to voicemail. I hung up. It was around 11 AM. He was usually up by now.

I was fed up and, looking back, probably in shock. It had been a week since our fight at the pool and Derek had not called me or returned my calls. I had tried to call him randomly, when I was bored tanning, but he never picked up. I felt like he had been purposely avoiding my calls and I hadn't done anything to deserve him treating me like that. I was so angry. I thought, *If he can't be bothered to pick up his phone for me when I need him the most, then I don't want him in my life.*

I got up and walked down the hall back to the waiting room.

"Come on, let's go," I said to Sadie.

We got in the car and she asked, "What happened?"

"I'm pregnant." I started to cry again. "And now I have to tell my parents. I tried to call Derek, but he didn't pick up."

Sadie shook her head. "I'm so sorry, Farrah."

"The nurse told me I can take a medication that will end the pregnancy, but my mom has to come in and sign a form first."

"Do you think your mom will sign?"

"I'm sure she will when I explain everything to her. Will you come in with me while I tell my mom?"

"Yeah, no problem."

We left Planned Parenthood and drove to my house. I was so nervous I was shaking. Since Derek wasn't there for me, I really needed to know that my parents would be supportive.

All the way home, I couldn't help thinking of the derogatory comments my parents had made about some of the teenage girls we knew who had gotten pregnant. I remembered my mom saying things like, "I would kick that girl out of the house if she was my daughter." I thought, *If I just tell them the truth, they should understand and at least let me still live with them.*

# TIME TO FACE THE MUSIC

When Sadie and I arrived at my house, my dad noticed right away that something was really wrong with me. The first thing he said when we walked in the door was, "Are you okay?"

I couldn't face my dad yet, so I muttered "Yeah," and kept walking. I wanted to talk to my mom first. I thought my mom would be more understanding and more helpful than my dad. Turns out I was wrong about that. My mom was working at home that day, so I walked into her office with Sadie following behind me. I was relieved I had a friend with me, but I knew this was going to be really uncomfortable for her. This wasn't her problem. She didn't even know my parents, but since Derek wasn't with me I really needed a friend by my side to give me moral support. I was still struggling myself with the reality that I was pregnant and I had no idea how my parents were going to react.

I couldn't stand keeping the news from my parents a moment longer. This was huge—it was life changing. So I took a deep breath and plunged in.

"Mom, we need to talk."

She was on a conference call, so she told me to sit and wait. I sat down. My mom was always busy working and I was used to waiting. But this was different. Every second that went by I felt a little more terrified to tell her that I was pregnant. I couldn't look at Sadie because my anxiety was growing and I knew the awkwardness of the situation must have been intense for her.

My mom finally finished her call and asked, "What's going on?"

"I have to tell you something. But just listen first and then we can talk, okay?"

I didn't want my mom to get upset and interrupt. I was already so emotional, I didn't know if I could handle hearing anything negative. I just wanted her to agree to let me end the pregnancy so everything would go back to normal.

My mom stayed silent. I took a deep breath and continued, "Mom, I just got back from Planned Parenthood. I took a pregnancy test and I'm pregnant. The nurse there said I can take a medication that would end the pregnancy. But you have to sign a notification form first since I'm not eighteen yet."

My mom was silent. She looked like she wanted to cry. She turned away and looked at her computer screen for a moment. Then she said, "God tells us to not kill any living being, and what do you think you're doing, Farrah? That medication works by cutting off nutrition and starving the egg."

"No mom, it's not like that. It's not even living yet. It's not a baby yet!"

My mom turned away from me. "No, Farrah. I'm not going to sign for something that kills a living being."

I was not ready to hear that being pregnant meant there was a living baby inside me. I wasn't allowing myself to let that sink in. I just wanted it to not be happening. I felt desperate and I couldn't understand why my mom was saying no.

I was confused. Nothing that was happening to me made sense. I had used birth control responsibly, but I was pregnant. My parents preached against teen pregnancy, but wouldn't agree to let me take a medication so I wouldn't be pregnant anymore. I couldn't even get the boy who got me pregnant to return my calls so I could tell him he was about to become a father. How was this happening? Why was it happening? I didn't understand my world anymore.

My mom didn't say anything else. We sat there in silence and I knew my fate was sealed. She wasn't going to sign. This pregnancy wasn't just going to go away.

I didn't say anything. I just walked out of the room and Sadie quietly followed me. I couldn't begin to imagine what was going through her head. I didn't know if she felt sad and embarrassed for me, or if she thought I was brave for telling my mom so directly. I didn't ask. I didn't want to talk anymore. She could tell I was freaking out, but there was nothing more to say than, "Bye. I'll talk to you later."

After Sadie left, I sat on the patio steps feeling sorry for myself. The same thoughts kept running through my mind: *I wish I had never got back together with Derek. I wish we had never had sex again. I wish I had gone to get a pregnancy test sooner. I wish I had just never had sex...*

For the first time, I thought about what my future would be like now. My mind was racing. *What am I going to do? I'm going to have to rely on my parents. I'm going to have to live here in their house. I have nowhere else to go. Will my baby have her dad around? Am I going to be able finish high school? What about college? What about my life?* One scary question led to a depressing realization, which led to another terrifying question, and on and on.

I started to cry sitting there on the patio steps, looking at the flowing pond under the tree. I thought, *I'll never be able to give my baby what my parents have given me, a stable house to live in, the clothes, the life she'll want to lead.* For the first time in my life, I truly appreciated how blessed I had been and now I felt like everything I had was about to come to an end.

After a couple of hours of crying, I pulled myself together and walked up to my room. My dad met me there. My mom had told him that I was pregnant and he was sad. He gave me a hug and said, "Farrah I want you to know that I love you and you can talk to me if you need anything." He wanted to talk more, I could tell, but I was so drained from crying and being confused that I didn't have the energy for an in-depth talk, so I told him I just wanted to go to sleep.

I was shocked by my father's reaction. He was so much more supportive than I ever thought he would be. I was relieved he still loved me and wasn't angry with me for getting pregnant. My parents left me alone for the rest of the night. I didn't know whether it was a good sign or a bad one, it was just very quiet in our house.

I decided that I would do whatever it took to gain back my parents trust so they would be supportive of me. I would show them that I was going to work hard, save up money, and be healthy during my pregnancy.

I called the nurse from Planned Parenthood and notified her that my mom wouldn't sign the form for me. From the moment I ended that call, I knew my life was going to be different.

# ON MY OWN

A couple of weeks later, I went to my first doctor's appointment. By then I had told my sister I was pregnant and she had helped me find an OBGYN. I borrowed her car and went to the appointment on my own. I knew couples usually went to these appointments together, but I still hadn't told Derek that I was pregnant.

After over a week of ignoring my calls, he had finally called me back but he didn't acknowledge that he had done anything wrong. He was still playing childish games, while I was trying to figure out how to grow up fast. I realized he wasn't ready to hear that I was pregnant. I felt like if I did tell him, he'd just let me down again. So when he called I acted like everything was okay and didn't tell him about the baby. I was sad that I was keeping such a huge secret from him, but if I was going to share this experience with him I wanted it to be on the right terms, so I held it in.

I kept the conversation short, and super casual. I didn't mention I was mad at him, or that I had called him a couple of days earlier. I could tell he was just calling me back to meet up like we usually did, but I wasn't ready to see him right then so I made up some excuse and got off the phone. Over the next few months, Derek would call me randomly, (and we did meet up a few times) but from that point on I began to distance myself from him.

I always, even when I was furious with him, wanted to see him, though. I always wanted to talk to him, or even just argue or yell at him, or stay on the phone in silence. I was caught in this place of wanting to be with him, but knowing that, if he wasn't going to change, the right thing to do was end it. So I just took things day-by-day, always hoping to find a way for us to get back on the same page. But as far as telling him that I was pregnant, I decided that I would wait until it seemed like he was ready to take on the responsibility of being a father.

Looking back, I can't help but question whether or not I made the right choice. Of course, if I had known he was going to die I would have told him about the baby—even if he was still partying and treating me badly. I would have taken whatever I could get. But these are the questions that haunt me: Would he have changed? Would he have still gone on hooking up with other girls, doing drugs, and drinking? Would we have been fighting and arguing all the time because I didn't agree with the choices he was making.

Would he have died anyway?

I'll never have the answers to these questions, but what I knew then was that I didn't want for us to be together just because I was pregnant with his child. I didn't want him thinking, *Well, I need to do the right thing and stick around because she's having my kid.* I didn't want him to resent me, or pretend he was changing and go on lying to me about what he was really up to. I wanted him to decide to be with me on his own. I wanted him to call me because he wanted to. I wanted him to choose to hang out with me because he would rather be with me than hang out with losers and do drugs and drink.

So I went to the appointment for the sonogram all by myself. I was sad that I was going alone, but in a way I was also proud of myself for taking responsibility and doing it on my own in a positive way. Walking in, I felt independent, like I was taking steps towards starting a new life, but I was also nervous because I knew this wasn't going to be like any check-up I'd had in the past. This appointment was really for my baby.

I changed into a gown and lay down on the table in the exam room. The nurse put the jelly on my tummy and I looked over at the ultrasound screen. My eyes were trying to focus and make sense of what I was seeing on the screen. It was crazy to be looking inside my stomach, knowing there was supposed to be a baby in there. I was trying to piece it all together and then suddenly it all came into focus. I could see this tiny peanut shape moving around the screen and my first thought was, *My mom was right. There is a little life growing inside me.* The ultrasound made me finally get it. I finally understood that I was carrying a living being inside my body.

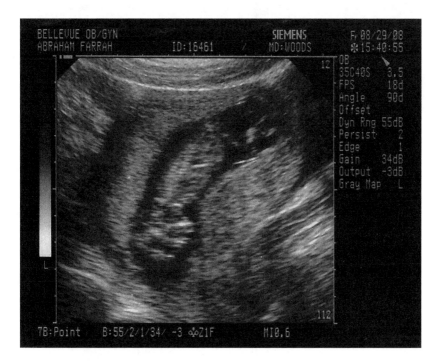

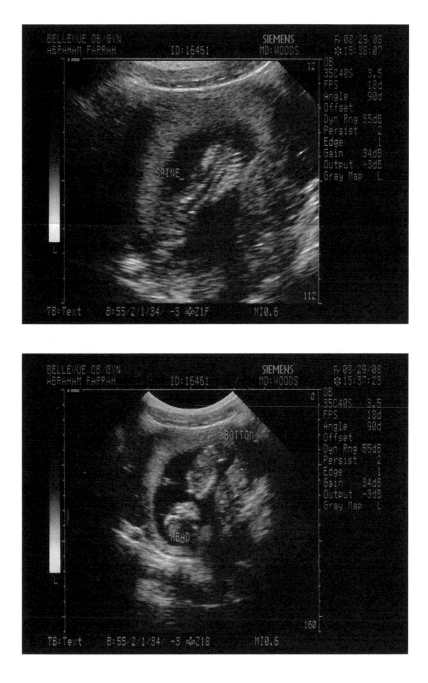

The nurse printed off some photos of the ultrasound for me. She said that I would probably start feeling the baby move soon and that in a few more weeks I could come back and find out if I was having a boy or a girl. Then she gave me some prenatal vitamins and some helpful advice.

I felt so different leaving the doctor's than I had when I arrived. My first instinct was to call Derek and share with him the amazing experience I had just had, but then I remembered my decision not to tell him about the baby. I thought about calling my parents, but I felt like they were still in shock and wouldn't really be able to understand my surprising happiness about what I had just seen. I was bursting with emotion but had no one to share it with. I was sad, but I shook it off and told myself, "I have a baby in me and I'm going to be healthy and take care of myself and do this right."

I did tell my sister about how the baby was developing and showed her the ultrasound photos. After that I put them in a drawer and saved them. I didn't have a baby book yet, but I knew I wanted to save them for my baby to see one day.

# CALLING ALL PREGNANT TEENS

Now that I knew for sure I was pregnant, I started going out less and less. I stopped hanging out with a lot of my friends, especially the ones that I didn't have much in common with other than partying. I focused on trying to graduate early, because I couldn't stand the thought of not finishing school before the baby came, but I was also trying to cherish the time I had left at school because I knew this period of my life was coming to an end. So I showed up to football games, cheered, went to practice, and tried to remain part of my old life for as long as I could.

I had been taking a six-month acting, modeling, and self-development course. I had always dreamed of working in the entertainment industry. It was something I was passionate about and I had worked hard at learning the skills I would need to pursue this as a future career. I'd even landed a great part-time modeling gig working as a ring girl for Omaha Fight Club, but, even though I still looked skinnier than most of the other girls, I was going to have to quit that soon since I couldn't be parading around in pumps and tight dresses once my belly got really big. I realized now that any offers for talent work would be out the door as soon as I started to show.

At first, I tried to hide from my instructors that I was pregnant, but then one day during a class break I decided to confide to my talent coach that I was pregnant. I could see the shock on her face. She was silent for a moment and then she said, calmly and in a very motherly tone, "I know you work really hard and try your best in class. I'll look around for other opportunities that might work for you now."

I was relieved. I knew it was a long shot, but at least she wasn't judging me and didn't say that I should just give up now that I was pregnant. Her offer to help me find other opportunities gave me hope and reassured me that I wasn't a complete failure. My parents and other people around me were acting like this shocking, unplanned pregnancy was going to define me—that suddenly all I would be was a pregnant, unmarried teen. I knew that wasn't me. I wasn't prepared to give up on my dreams.

At the next class, my coach took me aside and said that she had heard MTV was holding a casting for pregnant teens for a new show they were doing. She told me this was the best opportunity she had found for me because, honestly, there just wasn't a lot of work out there for pregnant teens.

That night I went to the MTV website, and there it was: a casting call for a documentary series about the experience of being a pregnant teen. They were looking to film teenage girls during their pregnancies through to the birth of their child. I told my mom and dad about the casting and they agreed to give their consent and help me make a video to send in to the producers.

Although I'm sure they had reservations about me being filmed for a national television show, I think at the time they were just happy to see me excited about something that would be like a job for me and take my focus off of Derek and being pregnant. At the time none of us knew how big the show was going to get or how enormous the impact on my life would be. I was just grateful that a door seemed to be opening for me.

The producers liked my video, so I began going through the interview process for the show. Initially, the casting agent would call me every afternoon and we would chat about what was going on in my life—school, friends, Derek, my parents, how I felt about being pregnant. It was nice to be able to talk to someone who didn't know me or Derek or my parents or any of my friends. I didn't have to worry that anything I was saying would become gossip.

It was like, even though I had never met this woman or even knew what she looked like, the casting agent was in some weird way turning into my friend. I think I really needed someone like her in my life at that point, since no one else in my life was open to talking and hearing me out without judging me. I didn't have to walk on eggshells with her, thinking she would tell my parents if I told her I had snuck out to see Derek. She wasn't one of my catty, gossiping cheerleader girlfriends who would spread my private business around at school.

I guess the casting agent liked what I had to say, because after a few weeks of those chats, I got to meet with the director, and she brought a crew to film me for a while, to see what my life was like—at home, at school, at cheer practice and at work. They still weren't sure the show would even go ahead, but they were going to use the footage they were colleting to make a reel for the show.

# WORD GETS OUT

It was good to see how filming would work if they ended up going forward with the show and it was fun working with the camera crew. On the first day of filming, they shot me cheering at a pep rally and during the day at school.

It was a long crazy day, with kids all over school reacting to the cameras being there; girls I barely knew or didn't get along with acted like we were best friends, some kids acted all crazy to get the attention of the cameras, while others wanted no part and steered clear of me. Whether they wanted to be on camera or not, it seemed like everyone was talking about he fact that MTV was filming at the school.

Because the show was brand new and still a secret, we didn't tell anyone the real reason the cameras were following me. We just told them MTV was filming for a show they were making about the life of a teenager. But as soon as filming started, rumors that I was pregnant began to spread like wildfire. Questions were flaring everywhere. People started staring, and even asking me outright if I was pregnant. I refused to acknowledge their questions, but the gossip reached a fever pitch. It was like a news flash: "Farrah Abraham

Is Pregnant!"

Word got back to Derek pretty quickly. Although it was difficult to cut myself off completely, I was really trying to distance myself from him. I knew that my parents wanted him out of my life and now that the cameras were around I had to be very careful about when and where I saw him. That part sucked, but I knew that, basically, my parents were right. This pregnancy had already limited my future prospects and I didn't need the drama of our relationship getting in the way of the one big opportunity I had. Not to mention the fact that I couldn't really tell him about the show since I hadn't even told him that I was pregnant.

A bunch of people must have called Derek and told him that cameras were following me around, because by the time I got home that afternoon, he was calling me to ask what was going on. As soon as I answered, he jumped right in, "Hey. So my friends told me you had cameras filming you today. Is that true?"

I knew there was no point in lying so I said, "Yes."

"Why are they filming you?"

"Why do you want to know? You don't share everything with me, Derek, so I'm not going to tell you everything."

"Well, some people are saying that you're pregnant. Is that true?"

I still wasn't ready to tell him, so I cut the conversation short. "Who cares what people are saying? I have to go. Talk to you later." And I hung up.

Meanwhile, the cameras followed me around at school, filming me with my friends and at cheer practice. At this point, I was trying to balance regaining my parents trust (since they didn't want me with Derek anymore) with maintaining a connection with Derek so that when he was ready to change we could pick up the pieces and be a family. I told my parents that I wasn't seeing him anymore and I made it clear to the producers that my parents weren't okay with Derek being a part of my story. I would avoid picking up his calls when I was filming. I never hung out with him or talked to him on camera, and I didn't tell my friends or family that we were still talking.

In those early days of filming, Derek called me non-stop. At first, I didn't answer—I just read his texts and listened to his voicemails—but he kept calling, demanding to know why they were filming and if I was really pregnant. He never asked if the baby was his, just if the rumor was true. It was like he was buying into the gossip like everyone else, and not that he had had a part to play in what was going on.

I hated that this was how Derek was asking me about the pregnancy; like once he had heard through the grapevine, then it was okay to ask me. He should have been the one person I was able to confide in, but he was only coming forward now that I had cameras filming me and rumors were all over the school. It sucked, but I tried to keep my head up.

I didn't want him to be just another person asking me or judging me. I wanted him to step up and say, "I know the baby's mine and I'm going to be there for you. I love you." But that never happened. The reality of my situation made me sad. Instead of having a close and loving relationship with my baby's father and him being emotionally supportive, he was only interested now that the gossip had started. That wasn't okay with me and it wasn't good enough for my baby.

Finally, one day, I couldn't take it anymore and I called him back. I was by the stairs in the basement at my house, so the cameras wouldn't see me, and no one would overhear. Derek picked up and asked what I was up to.

I kept it short. "Just trying to graduate."

Then he got to the point, "So I keep hearing you're pregnant. Are you?"

I didn't want to tell him. I felt like he didn't really care.

"No." I lied.

"Then why would everyone be saying that you're pregnant?"

"People like to gossip, I guess. I gotta go."

Derek started to say, "Why won't you talk to me?" but I hung up.

I felt like his last question was a no brainer. Why would I want to talk to someone who wasn't there for me? He should have shown concern for me months ago, when I called him from cheer camp and told him I had missed my period, instead of blowing it off like he had. Now, I felt like he was just harassing me to confirm the rumors like everyone else around me.

It went on like this for a while. Derek calling, demanding to know what was going on, and me sneaking around to call him back but avoiding telling him the truth. I should have cut it off with him completely, but, as hurt and as angry as I was, there was still a huge part of me that loved him and hoped he would change. I just wanted things to work out for us.

I didn't tell the producers when he would call, but I felt like they really wanted to catch me talking to Derek. They finally did film one of these conversations and, sure enough, he came across as jealous and crazy in that footage. I still have a hard time watching that moment. That wasn't who Derek really was. I hate that no one really knows what we were like when we were together and in love, before things got so complicated.

After the production crew left there was a month or so when everyone was in limbo, figuring out if the show was actually going to be made. In the meantime, I juggled a job, cheer practice, and early college classes.

# DONE WITH PROMS

I decided not to go to my prom. I had always dreamed of going to my Senior Prom—the perfect dress, the perfect date, the perfect night—but by the time I was a senior, my life was nothing like I had imagined it would be. I had already gone to two proms, was going to graduate early, and was pregnant with no boyfriend; not at all how I pictured my senior year would play out. My baby was due in February and prom was in May, so I could have gone, but I felt like buying everything I needed for prom would have been a waste of money. With a baby on the way, I needed to save that money for more important things.

So, instead I went to a homecoming dance with a guy friend of mine, who I had worked with at the restaurant. I had agreed to go because I thought it might be my last chance to go to a fun school dance, but I hadn't felt like dancing very much, probably because I was pregnant. Even though you couldn't really tell in my dress, I felt awkward; pregnant girls shouldn't be at homecoming, especially with some guy who isn't the baby's dad.

It was awkward for my friend, too. He kept probing me about who the dad was. All I wanted to do was go out and forget that my teenage life was about to end, so I ignored all of his serious talk and avoided his questions. We took pictures and hung out with some people—his group of friends. Since we went to different schools, I didn't know anyone at the dance, which was a nice change. I was tired of being in the middle of all the drama at my school. I tried to have a fun night, but in the end I realized I was just over the whole high school dance scene.

After homecoming, we didn't stay friends long because he still worked at the restaurant with Derek and that became an issue. I was sorry to lose him as a friend because he was one of the few guy friends I had left at that point.

I had quit working at the resataurant after I found out I was pregnant. I missed working there, but I didn't miss all the drama that came along with working with Derek. One night after I had gone out to to dinner with my friend, we stopped by the restaurant so that he could check his schedule for work. I decided to go in with him to say "hi" to the girls that I used to host with.

At first it was fun and exciting to be in there again, but that changed superquick when I saw my old manager. I had missed her, so I went up to her and said, "Hi, how are you?"

I was expecting a warm welcome, but instead she snapped, "You need to get out of here now! Leave!"

I was taken aback and shocked. "Why? What did I do?"

She gave me a look. "You know what you're doing. Leave!"

So I didn't say goodbye to anyone, I just walked out. My friend was still in the restaurant checking his schedule and he had driven, so I started walking to his car. I couldn't understand my old boss's reaction. I hadn't done anything wrong, but I felt like I wasn't welcome there anymore.

When I was halfway back to the car, I heard two guys yelling. It sounded like they were starting to fight. I looked back and saw Derek following my friend out from the restaurant. My friend walked up to me and said, "Keep walking," and we made a beeline for his car. Derek kept following behind us, yelling at my friend. He didn't even acknowledge that I was there, which pissed me off. He wouldn't acknowledge my presence, yet he wanted to fight my friend.

As we stopped to cross the street, Derek shouted, "Ah man, I just want to beat your ass."

I was so mad that Derek wasn't giving me any attention that I wanted to say something, anything, to piss him off. I started yelling, "Why don't you just do it then, Derek? But you're not going to do anything, are you? So shut up."

My friend shushed me, "Farrah, shhh! Just quit talking. I'm not going to fight."

As soon as we were able, we ran across the street, while Derek stood on the opposite sidewalk, still shouting threats.

When we got in the car, I asked what happened.

"Derek told the manager that we came in there on purpose to fight. He's mad because he thinks we're dating."

"Well, he could've asked me, instead of trying to fight you and getting me kicked out." I knew after this, my friend wouldn't want to hang out with me anymore. I thought about how stupidly Derek had acted. I just wished he had talked to me, instead of starting a fight. I wanted to explain everything to him, but I knew it would be a mistake to call him.

# FROM BAD TO WORSE

By October, the film crew had gone. They were waiting to get the green light on the show and were hoping to come back and film again when I was more visibly pregnant. At that point, I was almost five months along and, even though I didn't show enough for the cameras to pick up, my body was definitely changing. My belly was starting to poke out and I couldn't fit into my cute jeans anymore, so I had started wearing sweats and t-shirts every day. I hated dressing down and feeling like I was losing my cute little teenage body.

By now I was hating school, too. I was sick of being the center of gossip and just wanted to be done. I had no friends and I was short with people who tried to talk to me because I felt so disconnected from other kids my age. I didn't do anything like a regular teenager anymore. I went to school for half a day, went to work, took college classes at night and on weekends, and went to bed early most nights.

Now that my life had changed so much, I realized it was time to quit the cheer team. It all seemed so fake and hypocritical to me now. Our cheer coaches would preach leadership and doing the right thing, but it seemed to me now that the culture of cheerleading (which involves a lot of gossip and competing for popularity) was the opposite of that. It seemed to me to be a culture dominated by bitchy immature girls, obsessing over boys, causing fights, and acting cool. I felt mature enough to be a leader and take on real responsibility. So it was time to let all of that go.

Making that decision felt even more right after I got the news that the film crew had received the go-ahead to come back to finish filming for the show. One afternoon while I was at practice, my phone rang. I answered and it was one of the assistants from the production company calling with the good news. I was happy to have the opportunity to change my life, happy to be occupied with something constructive and positive, and happy to have something to take my mind off of Derek.

I was psyched that I was going to be on TV. It felt like the one good thing that was happening to me in what had been a very difficult fall. I knew I didn't want any negativity in my life and being on the cheer team had become a very negative experience for me.

The night I quit the cheer team, I went home and decided to throw away a bunch of my old high school photos and things that had a connection with that time in my life. I wasn't that girl anymore. I didn't have those same friends. I wanted to be free of that old life. While I was emptying out a drawer of old junk, I found Derek's swim goggles and some photos he had given me. Suddenly all the anger I had been swallowing came rushing up. I called Derek and told him to come get his stuff.

(I could have just thrown it all away, but honestly, I just wanted an excuse to see Derek. It had been a while and I missed him so much.)

Derek said he would come over and we hung up. My parents were downstairs in their room in the basement which is towards the back of the house, so I knew they wouldn't hear Derek coming in, and I justified that I didn't need to tell them that he was coming over just to grab his stuff and leave.

Pretty soon I heard him knocking on the front door. I let him in and we walked back up to my room on the third floor.

I said, "Here you go," and handed him his things. He looked at them and seemed to be a little bit taken aback that I was returning the photos.

"I'm not taking these back. You can just throw them away," he said.

"Fine. I will."

Derek knew I said that to hurt him, but he didn't get upset. He also didn't leave. Instead he leaned over and kissed me. It was like a jolt of electricity running through my body. I knew this was completely wrong. I should have pushed him away and told him to get out. But I was lonely and weak. I knew Derek wanted to have sex and I thought, *I'm already pregnant, so I have nothing to lose. I can't get more pregnant.*

I was totally about to cave, but before things could go much further, my dad walked in. Derek and I immediately sprang apart. I walked to the other side of the bed and Derek stayed where he was. I looked at my dad and it was like he had snapped. He had this crazy-eyed look, and he was holding a knife in his hand.

I was freaking out. I thought, *I'm pregnant and my dad is holding a knife and threatening my baby's daddy and now there is no chance of us ever getting back together.*

I said to my dad, "Michael, what are you doing with a knife?"

Derek grabbed our house phone. "I'm calling the police."

And then my dad pulled out his cell phone and he called the police, too.

It all happened so quickly. A minute later, the police arrived. My dad ran to the front door and began telling his version of what had happened. Then Derek told his version. Their stories didn't match up because both of them were lying. My dad said Derek was having sex with me, which, if given more time, could have happened, but hadn't. Derek said he came over to watch a movie, which was way off.

So I told the police what had really happened. They weren't happy with me for inviting Derek over and not telling my parents and they told Derek he was not allowed to be at my house ever again. But the worst part was that, since he had been holding a knife, they arrested my dad and took him to jail.

I was left to deal with the fallout, but I guess I was mostly to blame. About fifteen minutes later my dad called me from jail and told me to get my mom to come bail him out. Somehow she had slept through all the chaos and had no idea what my dad had done or that Derek had even been over.

I woke my mom up and told her what had happened, but she said she wasn't going to bail my dad out. From that I gathered that my mom and dad were probably in a fight. Since my mom wouldn't pay my dad's bail, I called Derek and told him he should pay it. I felt that this was really all his fault for trying to have sex with me in my house again. On the phone he sounded like he understood, so the next morning I waited for him to come get me before school so we could go bail my dad out but he never showed up.

I got a ride to school, but by lunch I still hadn't heard from Derek and now I had no way of getting home because my dad, who usually picked me up, couldn't drive me because he was in jail. My last class was PE, so I called Derek from the locker room to insist he come pick me up. I was past the point of being patient. I was pissed.

"Derek, where are you?"

"At home."

"Are you going to come get me?"

"No."

I snapped. "Derek, come get me. It's your fault my dad's in jail. I have no one to take me home. I've been waiting on you all fucking day!"

Derek had put me on speaker and I heard laughing in the background. I figured it was his sister and I was furious he was letting her laugh at me.

"It must be fun, Derek, hurting somebody who fucking loved you. It must be great doing drugs and wasting your life. FUCK YOU! If you don't get your ass here I will never talk to you ever again! You're the reason why there are all these problems in my life."

The school bell rang, and the other class was coming in.

"So are you going to come get me?"

He must have finally realized how angry I was because he said, "Yes. I'll be right there."

I needed to pull myself together. You could tell I had been crying and yelling. I looked up and saw that this girl I had known since junior high was in the locker room. I liked her, and she was one of the few people I still talked to.

She came up to me and asked, "Farrah, you okay?"

I told her I was fine. I knew that her boyfriend was friends with Derek, so I thought maybe she could give me some insight into what was going on in his life.

I asked her, "Have you seen Derek with any other girls?"

"No. He still talks about you sometimes."

I was surprised to hear that. It made me feel like maybe he was still in love with me. That was really all I needed to hear. "Oh? Well, we've been done for a while. I just wanted to know."

Then, for some reason, the whole crazy story came tumbling out, "He is so dumb. He came over last night to get some of his things and my dad got mad and pulled a knife on him and they called the cops on each other. So now my dad's in jail and I've been yelling at Derek all day."

She looked a little shocked. "Wow, I'm sorry." I could tell that she felt bad for me, but I don't think she really knew what to say or how to help.

I tried to smile. "Well, I guess it's all my fault anyway. I gotta go. See you later."

I went outside and walked in between the school building and the gym, down the railroad tracks, and then I finally saw Derek pull up in his maroon

Lumina—his baby. That car was his way to go anywhere he wanted, whenever he wanted. The sight of it made my blood boil. I was so angry I could barely look Derek in the face. I didn't even know who he was anymore. I was so angry I wanted to use him. I wanted him to have to pay for something since he hadn't come through for me on my dad's bail.

I got in the car and said, "Derek before you take me home, I need to stop at the drugstore."

He said, "Okay."

When we got to the drugstore, he parked and said, "I'll wait out here."

I told him, "No. You're coming in with me and you're buying my things. You didn't pay for my dad's bail so you're going to buy me something instead."

So we both went in together and I made him pay for a bunch of cosmetics and toiletries. The total came to fifty-something dollars. Derek turned to me and made a face, like it was too expensive, but I said, "Well, bailing my dad out would have cost a lot more." He pulled out his wallet to pay and when he took out the money he turned away from me so I couldn't see how much he had—so stupid. Then we got in his car and drove up the street to my house. He dropped me off in the alley at my back door, so no one would see us. He even tried giving me a kiss goodbye. I told him to call me later and got out of the car.

When I walked in the door to my house, my dad was right there to meet me. I could tell he was super angry.

"So, did mom come and get you out of jail?" I asked.

"No. I had to call a friend. Who brought you home?"

My dad looked like he went through hell in jail, and clearly still had quite a bit of hostility about it. I figured this was not the right time to be honest. It definitely wouldn't go over well if I said, "I made Derek come and get me from school because I wanted him to help me bail you out. But he wouldn't, so I made him buy me makeup instead and then he drove me home." I figured he knew Derek had brought me home anyway, so I just held that all in and kept walking.

After the arrest, Derek's mom insisted on pressing charges and things really began to deteriorate in my life. My entire family was mad at me for lying about seeing Derek and inviting him into the house that night. There was more pressure than ever to quit talking to him, especially now that the courts were involved.

I was sad and confused, but deep down I knew the break was needed. I couldn't handle much more stress. I felt like I was being forced to choose between my parents, who cared for me and were supporting me through this pregnancy, and Derek, whom I loved and was the father of my child. I didn't know what to do, but I knew I had to make a choice soon.

# IT CAME DOWN
# TO A LOST PHONE

It was a couple of days after the knife incident, and I was running late for gym class. I had been texting Derek to ask him to convince his mom to drop the charges against my dad. I had sent him a couple of texts saying, "You need to drop the charges" and "Why are you letting your mom do this?" and was waiting for his response.

I was running late for PE, so I sent one last text and then shoved the phone into my bag, which I stashed under the second bench in the locker room. Class had already started and no one was in the locker room, so I figured it would be safe. I always used to stash my bag under a bench if I was in a rush, which was most of the time.

After class, I hurried back to the locker room to check my phone for a text from Derek. I went to get my bag, but instead of finding it under the bench where I had left it, it was upside down in the middle of the room and all of my belongings were thrown everywhere; my makeup, bracelets, wallet, notes— you name it—all over the locker room floor.

At first I just stood there in shock, but then I remembered why I had rushed in—to see if Derek had texted me back. I started frantically gathering up my stuff, but my phone and bank card were missing. I went into a panic, searching and reorganizing my messed-up bag, picking up as much of my stuff from the floor as I could find.

I ran to the office to report what had happened and ask if the locker room security cameras had been on, but they hadn't. I called my mom and told her what had happened. I think she was used to hearing bad news from me by now, because she didn't seem surprised. She said we could cancel the bank card, no problem.

I asked her what I should do about the phone. It was the phone I had bought with Derek the day he left me at the pool. I hadn't gotten insurance on it and I didn't have the money to buy a new one. That phone seemed to have brought me nothing but trouble. Honestly, if I hadn't been so desperate to have a phone, I would have almost been glad it was gone. After all, that pool fight had led to me not telling Derek about the baby.

My mom offered me her old iPhone and said I didn't have to pay her for it. Her only condition was that I couldn't give Derek my new phone number. Reluctantly, I agreed.

And, just like that, my choice was made. Now Derek couldn't call me anymore and I couldn't call him, or he would be able to get my number. I understood why my mom was forcing me to choose. Lately he had seemed to bring me nothing but trouble; trouble my parents had to bail me out of, trouble I had to bail my parents out of—literally.

It was hard for me to stop trying to work things out with Derek. I really wanted to believe that I would see him at his best again. I wanted him to be like he used to be, when we first fell in love. I wanted him to be with me and our new baby, but I decided to accept my mom's deal and really keep my distance from Derek—at least for a while.

# THE LAST TIME I SAW HIM

Once I had made my decision to stop talking to Derek once and for all, I began to focus on getting my life on track. I was lonely, but more calm and positive now. I worked hard and got all A's and B's in both my high school classes and in my college courses.

With Derek out of the picture I thought the tension between my parents and I would go away, but now we argued all the time about the fact that I didn't have a car. They had become my chauffeurs and they were not happy about it. They would complain, argue, and get annoyed around the whole topic of taking me from one place to another. Hate started settling into our house.

Sometimes I couldn't help thinking, *Well, if we could just resolve things with Derek, then he would be driving me around right now like he used to.* But no, my dad had to pick me up from school every day, which was a huge inconvenience for him.

One day, I was waiting just inside the school for my dad to pick me up. I was wearing a pair of grey sweatpants and my cheerleading jacket—my staple outfit in those days. I was definitely stretching my dollar at this point; no getting a new winter coat, no splurging on clothes anymore.

When I saw my dad pull up, I ambled from the front door to his car. I didn't like to move too fast. I didn't want people to think I was trying to not be seen. Although I wasn't proud that I had gotten pregnant, I didn't want to give the impression that I felt ashamed either. I have always held my held high, and I wasn't about to let anyone think that being pregnant had knocked me down.

As I got in the car and shut the door, I looked over into the parking lot and saw Derek getting out of his friend's car. It was a two-door and he was getting out to let in this girl, who was rumored to smoke weed and get around. I recognized her from school. She was always probing me about what I was up to, and about my pregnancy. Sometimes I would ask her about Derek because they hung out with the same group of stoners.

I noticed Derek was wearing one of my big t-shirts that I had left at his house a couple of months back. I was disgusted and crushed. I had worn that shirt over to his house one morning when he had made me breakfast before school. That was one of those moments when we had been so happy, and I had felt good about us. It felt like he had deliberately chosen to take something good and cover it with a mess. However, as pathetic as it may seem, there was still this voice inside of me that was like, *If he's wearing my shirt, that must mean I'm still on his mind.*

I knew Derek must have seen me walking to my dad's car, since I had passed right in front of his friend's car, but he didn't acknowledge that he had seen me. I was filled with hate. I couldn't understand how he could just ignore me like that. Who could see their pregnant ex-girlfriend of a year and a half walk right by and just ignore her?

As I drove away with my dad, I felt like crying, but I held the tears back. Our lives were so different now. Derek was going out and partying all the time; he continued to be irresponsible and make immature choices. Here I was, in my dad's car, abiding by my parents rules. I didn't get to mess around.

I had to take everything seriously. One of us had to start being a parent. It felt like there was this line between us—you stay on your side and I'll stay on mine. I just wished it would stop being like that some day.

From that moment on, I began praying every night because I wasn't strong enough to deal with everything that was happening to me on my own. I prayed that Derek would get all of his immaturity out of his system so that when I had the baby we could come together and be in the same place in our lives. I prayed like this every night.

I didn't know it then, but that was the last time I would ever see Derek.

# CAKE AND HORMONES

Meanwhile, I had started taking cooking classes for college credit at a technical school a couple of blocks from my high school. I liked cooking because it was solitary. I didn't have to talk to people, so I didn't have to judge or be judged. Even though I still wanted to pursue modeling, now that I had a baby on the way I knew that I needed to get a degree so I had something to fall back on. I had always loved cooking and had a lot of experience working at restaurants, so I decided that getting a degree in Culinary Arts would be a good fit for me.

I focused on school and tried hard not to be stressed—besides worrying about saving up money for my baby—but sometimes my hormones got the best of me, especially when I was in class. I would look at other kids my age and see them wasting time or making stupid choices and I wanted to shake them and scream, *Don't you get that it can all change tomorrow? Don't you understand that there are more important things in life than gossiping and acting cool?*

When I looked around at other students in my classes, sometimes I felt like I wanted to rip all of them (even the ones I was okay with) apart. Looking back, I realize I was reacting to the stress of being a pregnant teen, of not having a supportive boyfriend, of having to be so dependent on my parents, but at the time I was so twisted up with emotion that it was difficult for me to hold back.

The stress just kept building and building until one day I finally snapped and lost it on a couple of girls in my baking class. It was the end of the course and we had to bake a cake during class for our final exam. I got to work and concentrated on making a great cake. When I was done, I glanced over at these two girls sitting near me. They had been sitting there, chatting and eating during the entire class instead of working on their cakes.

It pissed me off. I had worked my butt off and not wasted any time chatting so I could finish my cake. It made me angry that they thought it was okay to just do whatever and not get their final done. I knew it was none of my business, but I couldn't stop myself from saying something.

I walked over to them and snapped, "Do you think it's okay to just blow off the final? You should be taking this seriously, instead of sitting around talking and wasting your lives?" They just looked at me and didn't say anything, which annoyed me even more.

I stormed off and went right up to our teacher. I said that I thought it wasn't fair for them to just sit there and chat during the exam and I told her I thought she should talk to them. She nodded her head like she understood, but she didn't say anything to them. I was completely aggravated, but decided to drop it.

The next day in class, the two students I had been rude to surprised me with a huge cake that said, "Congratulations Farrah!" on it. They told me that they were proud of me for graduating early and explained that they had made this cake in secret for their final. That's why they hadn't been working on a cake the day before.

I was so surprised and touched by what they had done. It helped me realize that I had been trying to control everyone around me because my life was so out of control. I had no car, no independence. My life was moving in a direction I hadn't chosen for myself. I couldn't make Derek change, so I was angry with anyone who didn't behave the way I thought they should.

Take all that stress, add to it a teenage body raging with pregnancy hormones, and sprinkle the whole thing with a healthy dose of denial. Let these ingredients simmer for a few months and you will end up with a lovely little meltdown that will surely alienate friends and offend people.

I was grateful to these girls, not only for their sweet gesture and their support, but also for helping me see that I had been letting the stress and hormones get to me. I felt awful about yelling at them, but they understood where I was coming from and were supportive of what I was going through.

That was also my last day of high school and I blasted out of class that afternoon. I was so happy to be putting school behind me forever. One day I would be able to tell my daughter about how hard I had worked to graduate before she was born, earlier than everyone else in my class.

# THE WRECK

By December, I was really starting to show and had pretty much stopped going out altogether. The only talking I did with people was through Facebook or Myspace. Sometimes I would get messages from an old friend from junior high who was now good friends with Derek.

This kind of Internet socializing always led to issues and drama. I was pretty sure that he was either asking questions that were none of his business or that he was passing along messages from Derek. I wanted to hear from Derek—not his stupid friends—so I deleted all the messages without reading them. If Derek had wanted to reach out to me, he should have messaged me himself instead of having his friends bothering me and getting in our business. I hoped that since I kept ignoring his friends, he might get the point and reach out to me soon.

Christmas arrived and my family and I did the usual: got the Christmas tree out, decorated it, had a big family get-together, watched movies, and stayed out of the cold. It was a typical Christmas, except that this year I was pregnant and the presents I got were all for my baby. My mom and grandma got me a crib, my sister got me some children's books, and my dad got me baby clothes.

Although I knew that these presents were what I needed, emotionally I wasn't ready for baby things yet. Even though I was about to be a mother, I was still so young and it made me feel like I wasn't important anymore. I tried to be happy about all the baby stuff, but then I would think about how Derek wasn't sharing this experience with me and I would start to feel sad and lonely.

I hadn't heard from or seen Derek since he had ignored me in the school parking lot that day and I was starting to calculate how long it had been since we last hung out—about three months. If we went on not speaking for the rest of the pregnancy, by the time our baby was born it would be six months. That was the by far the longest we would have gone without speaking since that day I first met him at the basketball game.

By now my parents were convinced we were done for good. I acted like that was what I wanted, and I got so good at playing that part I was almost starting to believe it myself. Secretly, though, I hoped (and prayed) that once the baby came, Derek would change and we could be a family. Despite the drama, the lies, and the fighting, I still believed in him. I may have been about to become a mom, but really I was still just a teenage girl, trying desperately to hold onto her dream.

Two days after Christmas that dream died.

I woke up one morning and he was just gone. Forever.

My hopes for our family, gone. My happy ending, gone.

I still don't know exactly what happened that night. If Derek and his friend Zach, who also died that night, had been drinking before Derek got behind the wheel of the car or if it was just a fluke accident. After the initial shock wore off I just wanted to know how; how could this have happened?

For weeks after the accident I scanned the local papers and read every report, every interview his family gave about him.

*"Underwood's family said police told them Derek, who was the driver, may have tried to pass someone illegally on the road before hitting a patch of black ice."*

*"The family also said that they believe the three teenagers were drinking Saturday night."*

Mostly his sisters spoke to the reporters. Although I wasn't surprised by the things I read, I felt like everything they were saying about Derek was wrong, that they didn't really know him at all.

I read one article that said, *"Derek Underwood's sisters said that he was a good athlete and was about to be a father."* As heartbroken as I was, this almost made me laugh. As far as I knew, Derek wasn't involved in any athletics, unless you counted partying as a team sport. He wasn't even going to college like he should have been. The father comment made me furious because Derek had never stepped up to take on the role of father. I had been the one who had sacrificed and changed my life so I would be prepared to take on the responsibilities of parenthood, not Derek. Now I was going to have to be the mother *and* the father.

His sister was quoted saying, *"He would always cook for us, and all his friends, whenever they came to the house, he loved to cook, he was going to go to culinary school."* Yes, he would cook breakfast and he loved food, but I was the one going to school and getting my degree. He had told me he wanted to join the Air Force or work in real estate with his dad.

His other sister told reporters that Derek, *"Definitely lived on the edge, but he was responsible, he went to work, came home."* Sure he lived life on the edge, if you call weaving in and out of traffic, spinning a couple of times, and slamming into a pole living on the edge. The only edgy thing he did before that was that gas-and-go. In my opinion, Derek drank and took drugs not because he lived life on the edge, but because he was miserable and he used those things to avoid feeling the stress and emptiness of his life.

*"Police have not confirmed if the teenagers were drinking, wearing their seat belts, or how fast they were going when they crashed."*

I read later that the police found a bottle of vodka at the site of the crash, but, in the end, the autopsy showed that Derek's blood-alcohol level was within the legal limit.

In the end, what I'm left with is that Derek was the driver, the one in control. He lost control of the car, just like he lost control of his own life. He made poor choices that led him on the path that ended with the accident. But I also believe that everyone close to him had a part to play—including me.

I will never get over the fact that Derek died, but I also won't forget how things really were. I'm not here to sugar coat things, because what I believe is that if Derek had been more stable, he would have had the strength to make better choices.

**Source for this chapter:** Two Teens Declared Dead At Crash Scene  29 Dec. 2008
http://www.kcci.com/Two-Teens-Declared-Dead-At-Crash-Scene/-/9357770/7335346/-/bgiq52/-/index.html

# SEARCHING FOR CLOSURE

On December 30th, I went to Derek's funeral visitation. I contemplated not going, but I knew that if I had been the one who died I would have wanted Derek to be there for me.

After I had cried and cried and could think straight again, I couldn't stop thinking about going to see Derek at his visitation ceremony. But then I thought about all the issues this would cause. My parents wouldn't go with me, or anyone in my family for that matter, so that was out. They didn't want me to go. They felt it would just cause problems with his family and, of course, they were right,

The producers of *16 and Pregnant* wanted to film what was going on with me, but I didn't want cameras showing up with me to Derek's visitation. I had never had cameras around with Derek before and now it felt even more wrong. I didn't want to bring that kind of attention to his visitation.

As always with Derek, there were so many issues and it was all so complicated. I almost didn't go, but as the day wore on and the sun was going down, I felt like I was missing an opportunity. A couple of my girlfriends had offered to go with me, so I finally texted them back and asked them to take me.

I lied to everyone and said that I wasn't going, so the cameras wouldn't follow me to film and my parents wouldn't try to talk me out of it. Yeah, I know, lies are bad, but I wanted to go and not be bothered.

I knew his family and friends wouldn't want me there, so I snuck in at the last second. Outside the funeral home, I ran into his uncle, the one Derek had told me months ago had died. But here he was, very much alive. I couldn't believe it; even now that Derek was dead I was still being hurt by his lies. I wanted to be furious, but what could I do about it now? Yell at him at his funeral?

At that point I almost didn't go in, but I had already left my house and lied to my parents and the MTV crew about where I was going. I felt like I had gone this far, I might as well see it through. My girlfriends could tell I was hesitating, but they knew how much I needed to do this to get some closure and they encouraged me to go in.

So, I took a deep breath and we walked in.

It was a recently updated funeral home; clean and well lit, with warm pastel colors on the walls. It had that funeral-home smell, like a nursing home or hospital. I looked around to see who was there. It seemed to be a mix of random people: some kids Derek used to party with, and a bunch of people who were trying to act like they knew him, but who were really only there because of all the publicity. It was basically a shit show of kids who shouldn't have been there. I questioned whether they really cared about Derek or just wanted to be in on the drama.

I tried to go straight into the room where Derek's body was, but his sister came over to me and stood in my way. She demanded to know if the baby was Derek's. I felt like she was only asking to get a rise out me because she already knew the answer to that question. She'd already told the news reporters that Derek was about to be a father. I said, "No, it's not," and walked right past her.

I could feel everyone's eyes on me. Maybe they were shocked that I had shown up, maybe they thought my being there confirmed that it was Derek who had gotten me pregnant, maybe they thought I was going to start a fight. I didn't really care what they thought. I didn't want there to be drama at Derek's funeral. I just wanted to see him one last time, so I could wrap my mind around the fact that he was really dead.

I went up to the casket and looked at Derek lying there. I wanted to believe he wasn't really dead, just sleeping. Looking at him with his eyes closed, he looked just like he did when he would fall asleep beside me and I would stare at him in the darkness of my bedroom. But this time his eyes weren't going to open. He wasn't going to tell me he loved me anymore, or lie to me anymore, or do anything ever again. He was dead.

I turned and looked over at the video they had made for the visitation. Derek's school photos, snapshots of him with friends, and family photos faded in and out on the screen. When our prom pictures came up I was shocked that they had even included photos of me, but I was grateful that they did.

I sat down with my girlfriends, but I couldn't let my guard down and just soak in this last time I would ever see Derek because his sister began complaining loudly about me to her stepfather, saying she wanted me to leave. Then a bunch of her friends lined up in front of Derek's casket and the video screen, so I couldn't look at him anymore. I didn't want to be part of a big dramatic scene, so I just got up and left. To me, what she was doing was incredibly disrespectful.

Despite the confrontation with Derek's sister, I was happy that I had gone. After I got back home I remembered a time when I got so mad at Derek that I told him angrily on the phone. "When you die, I'm not even going to show up to your funeral." I deeply regretted ever saying that and I felt that by going to his visitation I could somehow show him I hadn't really meant that. I thought about how immature we were and the time we wasted with our dumb fights. I loved Derek and, even if it meant lying to everyone, it felt right to have been able to see him one last time

It was awkward though. My parents knew I had gone out around the time of Derek's visitation. That night, they were not-so-casually hovering around me to see if I would talk. The producers from *16 and Pregnant* double-checked with me to see if I had gone. I told them I hadn't. I figured I should just stick to saying no. I didn't really want to talk about it with them, anyway. This was my personal time, my last day with Derek—not theirs. I didn't want to share.

# LIFE GOES ON...

As time went by, I had no choice but to set aside my sadness and move on with my life. I was about to become a mother and it took all of my emotional strength to process all the traumatic changes being pregnant had brought to my life.

Losing Derek, so suddenly and violently, was too much to bear. So I kind of went into denial about it. It was less painful to act like I was just still not talking to him. My family never brought up what had happened and we never talked about him, so it was easier to get through my days pretending Derek and I were still in a fight than face the reality that he was never coming back.

But every day when I woke up, even sometimes in my sleep, memories of our past would come to me like they were real. I would be transported back to the times when he would sneak into my room and spend the night with me, when it was just the two of us and we were so happy together. In those moments I could almost feel him holding me in the night, hear him whispering in my ear, "I love you, don't ever forget that." It brought me to tears every time, and in those moments I couldn't ignore that Derek was really dead.

I kept quiet to everyone about missing Derek. I didn't talk about it at work, or at school, and I definitely didn't talk about it at home. I stuffed my grief way, way down and put on a brave face for my family and for the MTV cameras.

I postponed my baby shower as long as I could, since I wasn't much in the mood for a party, but two weeks before my due date I looked like I was ready to pop any minute, so my mom invited a few close friends, my teachers, a few neighbors, (the MTV cameras) and my immediate family to her house for the shower. When everyone showed up, it was all smiles and showering me with gifts. I tried my best to be bright and happy, to make sure everyone was having a good time, and to show that I was grateful they had all come. But mostly I felt hot, lonely and uncomfortable,

I got everything I needed and more, so much, in fact, that I didn't have enough space in my room to put it all. I felt so lucky to get practically everything I needed. It helped to relieve a lot of the financial stress I was feeling at the time. At this point, I was at college taking classes all day, and at night on the weekends. I also was working thirty hours a week, serving and hosting at Applebee's. I was trying to save up for baby expenses, hospital bills, and to pay for the culinary classes I was taking.

During the shower I was able to avoid thinking about Derek, but reality hit hard after everyone went home. I was organizing all of the new baby presents in my room; stacking diapers and folding baby clothes. I wanted to be able to say, "Derek we don't have to worry about buying a baby bed, clothing, diapers, etc.," going down the whole list, but instead I was thinking, *I'm so grateful my friends and family got me everything I needed, so I won't have to work as much now.*

When I finished organizing my closet, I stood back and thought, *This used to be my room growing up, when I was a kid and playing with toys. This room was where Derek and I used to be in love. Now this room is a baby nursery.* It was a lot for me to process. Everything had changed so fast.

# PREGNANT GIRL

On top of all that, being pregnant was wearing me out. Suddenly things that had always come easily to me were physically exhausting or just plain awkward. If I stood for too long, my legs would swell and my back would start to ache. My OB told me that I needed to be more careful about pushing myself too far, that I shouldn't stand for long periods of time—which is next to impossible when you're working in a kitchen and running around a restaurant all night. This was hard for me to take. I was used to being strong and fit, so it came as a blow to my pride that my body was making things tough for me.

Even simple everyday things had become difficult. Suddenly, cutting and chopping for my culinary classes was a challenge. Instead of being able to stand next to the table edge, like every other chef in training, my pregnant belly stopped me about a foot away from the food I was working on. Then, for stability, I had to stand with my legs shoulder-width apart in a sort of squatting position—not the most attractive (or comfortable) pose.

Worst of all was how sick being near heat made me feel, which is problematic when you are sautéing, frying, and boiling all day. There were times when I felt like I was going to pass out or vomit right in the middle of class. I had no choice but to suck it up and push through, but I was miserable and honestly there were days when I was ready to quit. But then I would remember how I felt about cooking before I got pregnant; effortlessly cutting, cooking, keeping up with the pace and enjoying every second of it. I realized making a choice as big as changing my major would need to be put off until after the baby was born.

I also had to be more careful about what I ate and about keeping myself hydrated or I would get bad heartburn and stomach aches. Things like greasy food at restaurants gave me heartburn. It was horrible and antacids didn't help. But the single worst food that my body would instantly reject was bananas. It was so bad. One day I was in class eating a banana and within seconds it was forced from my stomach and back up and out as banana puke; so gross. I quit eating bananas right then and there.

The pregnancy also wore me out mentally. My mind was foggy, I had a hard time focusing, and it became hard for me to retain information. Everyone in class started calling me "pregnant girl." I was huge and ready to pop and, honestly my mind was elsewhere, so I just let it go. I hated being defined by my pregnancy, but I also understood it wouldn't be for much longer.

# HELLO SOPHIA!

Although I knew by this point that I was having a girl, I hadn't picked a name yet. One night, my mom, my grandparents, and I went out to dinner. I had looked into Italian names because my family is very fond of our Italian heritage, but my top picks were Saychelle, Melania, and Audrina. None of these were very Italian, and when I shared them, my family shot me down with some pretty negative comments.

Since they were all helping me so much with my pregnancy, I thought, *Why not let us all choose the name?* So together we agreed on Sophia Laurent Abraham, after my favorite actress, Sophia Loren.

Now my baby had a name. From that moment on I began to think of her as Sophia.

My original due date was the 28th of February—but I was pretty sure I was going to have Sophia before then. Still, I was I really was hoping to hold her in until February 25th so I could get my finals done. No such luck.

On the night of February 22nd, 2009 I watched the Oscars with my mom We saw Sophia Loren walking the red carpet and she looked beautiful; tan skin, chic make-up, healthy brown hair, and a gorgeous dress. It was a happy reminder that the inspiration for my daughter's name was a successful, talented, and beautiful role model.

I drank my soda pop, finished watching the awards show, and went to bed. Just as I was falling asleep, I felt warm liquid suddenly leaking from between my legs. It felt like I had peed, but I was pretty sure that wasn't the case.

I realized, with a little panic, that my water had broken. I grabbed my cell phone and called my MTV producer. I had promised that if my water broke in the middle of the night I would call right away. Within minutes, the camera-woman had jetted over from her hotel and was at the door. I was waiting in my bed, with the lights off, and finally my mom came upstairs and turned the lights on. She took one look at me and said, "Oh yeah. Your water broke. It has that smell." I had to laugh because all I could think was that the smell reminded me of having Derek's cum inside me. I couldn't really share that with my mom, though, so I kept that thought to myself.

So this was it, I was going into labor. I called my sister and told her to meet us at the hospital, but she was sick and we didn't want to risk her passing anything on to Sophia, so we decided she shouldn't come to the hospital. My grandparents were out of town and my dad was living an hour away for work at the time. So in the end it was just me, my mom, and the camerawoman.

I went to the bathroom to change my pajamas, which were now com-pletely soaked. There seemed to be an endless supply of fluid running down my legs. There was so much liquid. It wouldn't quit. I peed, hoping that might make it stop, but it kept right on running down my legs. By the time I got to the hospital, my pants were soaked again. This was not how I pictured going into labor would be. I don't know what I expected, but it had never occurred to me that it would start out so soggy.

We arrived at the hospital around two AM and I was checked in and assigned to a labor room. My mom got comfortable, while I changed and sat down on the bed and tried to take it all in. My doctor had been out of town and wouldn't be able to get to the hospital until ten AM that morning. This was not how I pictured it would go down. I had assumed my doctor would be waiting at the hospital for me and that I would deliver the baby immediately.

At around four AM, I finally started having contractions. They were so intense; my head started throbbing with pain. This was not the kind of pain you could shrug off. It was engraved into my brain. I tried to rest until my doctor got there, but I wasn't sure how much longer I could stand the pain. The contractions became unbearable. The pain took over my head. I didn't feel it in my stomach or back or crotch or anywhere else—just in my head. It got so bad that I couldn't stand hearing my mom's voice anymore, or the nurses, or cell phones ringing, or people talking in the hallway—any sounds at all really.

I was so aggravated I could barely look at anyone, but it was mainly my mom's voice that I remember driving me crazy because she kept chattering away. At one point, I snapped and I told her I couldn't stand to hear her voice anymore and to get out. She sat quietly in the corner of the room until I got my sanity back.

By this point I was like, *Okay, it's go time. Let's get this baby out!* But the nurse told me I wasn't ready, besides my doctor wouldn't be there for another couple of hours. I was losing my mind. The pain was so intense. Everyone trying to sooth and calm me was only aggravating me more. Finally, the nurses suggested I have an epidural and I agreed. The epidural needle went in and for a moment the pain got worse, but then it seamlessly went away.

After that I felt much better and settled down to wait for my doctor to arrive. When he finally got to the hospital, I was ready. With the pain gone, I was able concentrate on breathing and preparing to push. Since I hadn't taken any birthing classes, I was surprised to find that I was a natural at doing the birthing breathing.

I was praying that I didn't have to get a C-section. That was my biggest fear. The idea of having my stomach cut open completely freaked me out and, honestly, I was also worried about my body getting back into shape, for modeling. I wanted my six-pack abs and tight butt back again. But I also knew that however the labor needed to be for my daughter, whatever the doctor recommended was best for her, that I would agree with him. I was just praying everything would go smoothly.

Thankfully it did. When it was time to push, the nurse held my left leg and I held my right leg and the doctor helped me get through the pushing. He had to let me know when to breathe because I couldn't feel anything from the epidural. It was great to not feel pain, but the numbness made it that much harder to push. I heard my doctor say, "Push one last time," and even though I was exhausted I took a deep breath and pushed as hard as I could.

That did it. On Feb 23rd, at 10:25 AM, my baby girl was born. My doctor said I did great and while he was sewing me up, since I had torn a little during the delivery, the nurses took Sophia to check her out and clean her up. I watched them weigh her and give her a bath. When I heard her crying, I instantly felt like a protective mom. Just a moment ago she had been in the warmth and safety of my protective womb, now she was being bathed and handled for the first time and she clearly was not happy about it. I couldn't wait to hold her.

As soon as the nurses were done and Sophia was all swaddled and clean, they handed her to me. I had never held a baby before. I thought I would be clumsy and awkward, but she felt so right in my arms. She looked up at me, all quiet and content now, and I could tell she instinctively knew that she was safe and back with her mom.

Looking down at Sophia for the first time, I instantly saw Derek—the shape of her face, the dimple on her chin, her eyes—all Derek. For the first time in so long, I was happy. I felt like he was there in some form, seeing our baby with me. I have never been so intensely happy and so deeply sad at the same time in my entire life.

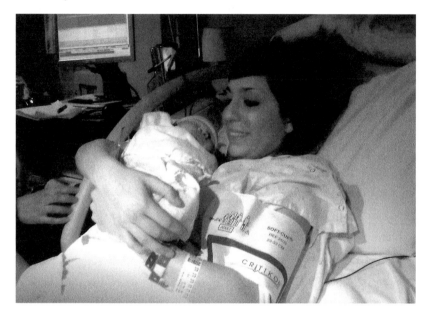

My mom was by my side through the whole delivery. She even cut the umbilical cord, which is hilarious since she had always been so squeamish even just talking about the birth. She told me later about cutting the chord. There had been so much going on and I had been so exhausted, I hadn't even noticed. Giving birth was an amazing experience, but it took everything out of me—emotionally and physically. I was just so happy and relieved that everything had turned out okay. More than okay. Sophia was perfect.

Later my dad, grandparents, and friends came to the hospital to see me and meet the baby. It was great to see everyone and they all fell in love with Sophia. I could tell that some of my friends that stopped by didn't get it; that I had just given birth and that my baby and being a mother was more important to me now than acting cool and listening to gossip, so I kept those visits short. All I really wanted was peace and quiet—and sleep, lots and lots of sleep.

# BRINGING HOME BABY

Now that I had given birth and I wasn't actually pregnant anymore, I was completely shocked by my body. I felt skinny and weak, but with a jiggly tummy. And there was so much blood. Every time I went to the toilet and saw how much blood was coming out of me, I felt like I must be bleeding to death. Once the stitches from where the doctor had sewn me up down by my crotch started to heal, they became itchy and uncomfortable. I had thought dealing with the changes to my body from the pregnancy was hard, but this was a whole new level.

Another thing I didn't know about until it happened was how painful it would be when my milk came in. My boobs were so sore. I thought I was having a heart attack or bad heartburn, but the nurse explained to me that this was normal when your body is getting ready to produce milk for the baby.

After two nights in the hospital we were ready to go home. Before Sophia and I could be released I had to watch a movie about going home with a new baby for the first time and postpartum depression. I also had to learn how to buckle Sophia into her baby car seat. It was a process, but I finally got it.

When my grandpa finally drove Sophia and I home, I was relieved but terrified. In the hospital, the nurses were there to help me take care of Sophia. If anything went wrong, experts who knew what to do surrounded me. It was scary to be going home, knowing that kind of support wasn't going to be there anymore.

My mom and my dad tried to be helpful, but Sophia was very much my responsibility. It was hard getting her to sleep. She wasn't eating, and when she did she would instantly puke it back up. A week went by with no sleep. Sophia started losing weight, and I was so worried about her.

My mom didn't get it. She was convinced I had postpartum depression. She kept making comments that I was crying and being emotional for no reason. She couldn't understand that I was emotional because I was worried about my child not eating and that I was exhausted from not getting enough sleep. I was freaking out because I didn't want my child to die on me—the way her father had. I wanted to say, *If I am depressed about anything, it's about Derek being dead, and that I feel like my baby might die on me right now.* But I kept my mouth shut and hoped she would eventually just leave me alone.

To help Sophia keep her food down and start putting on weight, the doctor suggested we switch to a formula that would be easier for her to digest. I also decided to try breastfeeding. When I was pregnant I was convinced that I wasn't going to breastfeed. It had seemed so weird to me and people (like my mother) made it sound like it would ruin my boobs. Now it felt like breastfeeding was a matter of life and death. Nothing was more important to me than Sophia's health, so I gave it a shot.

Sophia really took to the breastfeeding, and as long as she was happy I was okay, but I couldn't see myself doing it for too long. To me it seemed like extra work—wearing special clothes, having milk leaking all over my shirts. It wasn't for me. I liked that my boobs were bigger, but that was really it for me.

I told my mom that Sophia and I needed to sleep downstairs with her so she could help me out at night. I needed some sort of help badly, but it didn't work out as I had hoped. My mom was beginning to crack from the stress of helping me and when I went to feed Sophia in the middle of the night she would start arguing with me about random things; driving me to school, my work schedule, things she was mad at my dad about, her bills getting more expensive.

At three o'clock in the morning, I couldn't handle so many argumentative topics, so I would just block her out, but when I didn't answer her she would just get angrier. I couldn't handle it. She was driving me nuts and I wasn't getting any extra sleep, so Sophia and I moved back upstairs into my room.

When I stopped nursing Sophia, my boobs began hurting again. They would get so painfully engorged that even showers became a painful experience. The water made my boobs get really hard and my muscles would tense up. That lasted until my milk finally dried up.

It was so overwhelming how my body was changing, how my life had changed, how my relationship with my parents had changed. I just wanted to get back some control over my life.

# PARTY GIRL

Two and a half weeks after Sophia was born, I went back to work at Applebee's. Diapers and baby formula were expensive, and I knew after a while my parents would get fed up with having to pay for everything.

I needed the money, but I also needed to get out of the house. I wanted my independence back and to be out there in the world again. I went back to school and started working more and more. I wanted to save up for a car and not have to put up with all the complaining from my parents.

After two months, I finally got my own car and that helped a lot. I think that took a little of the stress off my parents, too. Now I could take Sophia out and we could have our own time together. I would take her to the park and show her the places that her dad and I had gone together.

By the time Sophia was three months old, my life was starting to settle into a relatively normal routine. I decided to try dating again. It had been so long since I had gone on a date. I was lonely and I thought that if I started going out a little bit, maybe I it would help me move on and get over Derek.

But as soon as I started dating again I felt horrible, like I was a bad mom for going out. My parents got on my case, which made me feel worse. Any time I told them that I was going on a date or just out with friends, they would make me feel guilty for not staying home with Sophia and accuse me of taking advantage of their help.

On top of that, I got a little insecure about my body, literally everything from my face to my tummy, to my legs. I was always second-guessing: do I look good enough? Even relatively innocent comments made me feel insecure. One night, I went out on a group date with some friends. When I got up to go to the bathroom, one of the guys said, "Look at that booty." I was still in my post-pregnancy "fat jeans" at that point and I thought, *Oh God, my butt is out of control.*

I wasn't comfortable with myself, so I dated random guys but I didn't pay much attention to them because I was working, going to school, trying to spend as much time as possible with Sophia, dealing with the stress of living with my parents, and taking on the role of a single mom.

I was partying too much; going out to just drink, mingle, and escape the stress of my life. It quickly became an issue. I would tell my parents that I was going out with friends to hang out, because I wasn't old enough to drink, but they knew that I was lying because I was coming home at two or three AM every weekend. There was no getting around the truth that I had gone out to party.

My parents saw it as a problem, which I understand now, but at the time I couldn't stand being around them. I hated them hovering over me, criticizing me and trying to control how I was parenting Sophia and how much I worked and went out. I felt like they were always in my business. I needed an escape and at the time I felt like a couple of hours out with my friends on the weekend was what I needed and deserved.

One night, I finally realized that being a party girl wasn't who I really was. I had met up with my weekend friends and we went downtown to some bars and clubs. I drank too much and did some coke. I had been partying a lot, but this was a whole new level for me. I couldn't handle the effect of the alcohol and drugs. I started crying about Derek to some guy I was kind of into, and everything I had been holding down for months came spewing out of me like vomit.

To make matters worse, after being an emotional basket case and telling this poor guy about how I was still in love with my dead ex-boyfriend, I suddenly got angry and started yelling at him about how he wasn't like Derek. The next morning I woke up looking and feeling like a mess, and my nose hurt from the coke. I'm not proud of this episode, but it was a good wake up call for me. From that night on I quit partying. I can look back at it now as something to learn and grow from.

But the complaining from my parents continued. They told me I was sleeping too much, that I wasn't communicating with them about my schedule. I sank into a depression. I started crying a lot at night and just wanted to be left alone. I was dating, but I didn't really care about the guys. I wanted to be in a relationship so that I didn't feel alone. But everything was wrong.

# THE BREAKING POINT

There were days when it felt like I was taking on the role of six different people. I was a mother, a daughter, a girlfriend, a student, an employee, and a teenager all rolled up in one exhausted and confused package. Then at night I would think about Derek and become just a lonely girl with a broken heart.

Often, though, the hardest part for me was just being a daughter. I resented my parents for having caused so much stress between me and Derek. I resented them for telling me I couldn't see him any more. At the time I blamed them for a lot of the problems Derek and I had experienced, but now I can see that I was directing a lot of anger at them because I had nowhere else to put it. The fact that I was living with them and completely dependent on them made it all the more stressful.

I definitely had some hate towards my parents in those days, especially when they started having issues and talking every day about getting a divorce. I didn't want to hear it. This had been going on my whole life and I was sick of it. It seemed like they would fight and my dad would move out and then they would make up and he would move back in again. They were always on and off, always traveling and not spending much time together.

I felt like they should have gotten a divorce when I was way younger. They had major fights and issues, but they didn't want to go to counseling. I now suspect that the only reason they stayed together as long as they did was for me, because as soon as I turned eighteen and was out of the house they got divorced.

I think their rocky marriage has a lot to do with why I always believed Derek and I would eventually get back together. To me the cycle of fighting, breaking up, and getting back together was normal in a relationship. It never occurred to me then that these were serious signs that a relationship is not going to work.


Having the baby in the house brought my parents together for a little while, but by the time Sophia was almost a year old, it seemed like they were arguing all the time again. I was already over it the day their fighting started up again. Just like they had told me to quit talking to Derek, I felt like telling them to quit talking to each other, but I knew it wasn't my place. I just didn't want to be around it anymore or hear about it anymore and when they fought around Sophia I really couldn't handle it.

One afternoon, when it was gray and cold outside, my parents began fighting in the car. My dad and I wanted to go get groceries, but Sophia was sleeping and I didn't want to wake her up. We asked my mom to watch Sophia, but she didn't want to because she wanted to study for her executive MBA program. She got angry, got out of the car in the driveway and went into the house and locked the door. I took Sophia out of the car and my dad left.

I unlocked the door and went inside. My mom was in the kitchen, talking loudly. I said, "Sophia is sleeping," meaning, *Shut up before you wake her up*. My mom kept talking and trying to get at me, so I left the room. As I was walking upstairs, I saw that she was going through my mail. I got pissed.

I had told her many times not to go through my mail. I didn't have anything to hide; it just felt like an invasion. It represented everything about living with my parents that was driving me crazy, how they never gave me space or stayed out of my business.

I snapped, "Get out of my mail!" and she got mad and threw a shirt that I had gotten in the mail at me. I was holding Sophia in my arms and the shirt hit her and frightened her. I sat Sophia down in the other room, because I felt a fight coming on with my mom and I didn't want Sophia to be around it.

I went back to the kitchen to get the rest of my mail, but she refused to give it to me. It got physical, punches were thrown, hair was jerked, and threats were made. I had my mom to the point where I was holding her and she was saying "Ow" and "Let go." I knew at this point I was way too angry, so I grabbed Sophia and went upstairs. I laid her down and that's when I looked in the mirror and saw my face. My lip was busted and bloody, and I thought, *I don't want this around my child.*

My mom had always had these damn selfish fits with my sister and I. Now it had escalated to punching, and Sophia had been caught in the middle of it. Enough was enough. I wanted to send my mother a message that I wasn't going to take her overbearing, controlling selfishness anymore, so I called the police.

After I made the call, I waited upstairs in my room. Maybe five minutes went by and then I heard a knock on the front door. I walked out of my room and down the front staircase. My room was right by the front door, but my mom had rushed to the door so fast that she beat me there. I was still walking down the stairs, when I heard the click and swish of the front door being unlocked and opened.

I was expecting to hear the routine sound of an officer saying, "We received a report of a fight, what seems to be the problem?" Instead, I heard what sounded to be an introduction that got cut off, and man's voice yelling,

"Put the knives down!" By the time I got to the door, I saw an officer holding a gun pointed directly at my mom

I said, "What's going on? Put your gun down."

The officer said something like, "Your mom needs to put down her knives. She won't put down her knives!"

I looked over at my mom. She was standing there holding two knives, one in each hand. "Mom what are you doing with knives?" I asked and, again, the officer yelled, "Put your knives down!"

She didn't move.

I said, "Mom put the knives down!"

At this point I was truly terrified because, from what I was seeing, my mom was about to get shot in the head because, for some reason, she couldn't just put the knives down.

This was out of control. I said one last time, "Mom put your knives on the ground." Finally, something in her brain clicked. She put the knives on the ground and the police officer lowered his gun. In seconds the police had my mom restrained. She was yelling "Let me go," and "Farrah, look at what you've done."

She was blaming me for what was happening to her, but I was thinking, *You almost got yourself killed because for some unknown reason you rushed to open the door with two knives. Even if they weren't cops what the fuck were you thinking?* I truly felt bad for my mom. But I felt like she had gone so far off the deep end that she really need a reality check to learn how to treat others, quit fighting, quit manipulating, and begin acting like the parent I needed her to be.

I was in such shock that it all almost seemed to be happening in slow motion or somewhere far away. I snapped myself back into the scene in our front room when one of officers began asking me questions about the fight I had had earlier with my mom. As this point I was so taken aback by what had just happened that I had almost completely forgotten about our fight, which was the whole reason the police were there in the first place.

The officers were trying to piece together what had happened, but my mom was hysterical. She was so worked up that no positive progress could be made at this time, which wasn't working for the police. They had to make the choice, so off my mom went to the cop car, and to jail.

One of officers drove off with my mom, and the others stayed behind to ask me questions about what happened between my mom and myself that had led to our physical altercation. They took photos of my face, where my lip had split, the area where we had fought, and the knives she had in her hands. After that they left.

I stood there in total shock. I didn't know what to do now. I was pretty sure I was going to need to find a new place to live. I was just relieved that Sophia was sleeping and taken care of. What had just happened seemed like the most awful thing I had ever experienced (and I had experienced quite a bit by then) but little did I know that in the days and weeks to follow, I would see the worst time in my whole life between my family and I.

# THE AFTERMATH

———··◁∞▷··———

The next day, I was contacted by a social worker from the Department of Human Services. They told me they would have to take Sophia into protective custody if I kept living with my mom. Our family's attorney, whom I've know all my life, and the chief criminal justice attorney from the courthouse also called to talk about what was going on with my mother and about the charges against her.

I dropped the charges, but they still said that my mom could not be around Sophia unless a third person was present to chaperone, which meant that we couldn't live together anymore. I hoped my mom would move in with my grandparents temporarily, so that I could stay at our house with Sophia until I figured out what to do, but she couldn't admit that she should have handled things differently and insisted that I be the one to move out.

I asked her, "Where do you expect me to go now? I have to move out since you want to come back here. I can't rent anything because I don't have enough money saved or time to find an apartment." I had nowhere else to go, so I said I was going to have to stay in her rental apartment in the house that she owned across the street.

My mom still wanted to be in control. She acted like my moving into that apartment was a big sacrifice. Her response was, "So you want to move into my house across the street, I suppose I will let you, but there will be rules…" and so on, blah, blah, blah. I felt like after what had happened, she should have been more apologetic. I had dropped the charges against her, so her ass could get back into her house. I was making it easier for her, but she was still being controlling and adding to the distance she had already created between us.

My dad was mad at me for calling the police. As usual, my mom was yelling at him, acting like this was his fault for, you know, the way I was acting. This was typical for them whenever we had a big blowout in our house. My mom would act like the victim and manipulate others into thinking they were the problem and my dad would cave in to her instead of resolving things the right way.

This time I wasn't going to let that happen.

I told him he shouldn't have left me the day my mom and I had the fight. He was always taking off to avoid conflict with my mom and then getting drawn back and bullied into taking her side. I knew I had done the right thing in calling the police. Even after I had dropped the charges the police still made her do community service and take anger management classes, which was exactly what she needed.

I was being a parent and putting my daughter and her wellbeing first. It was my parents who, at this time, had gotten caught up in their issues and the stress of what we were going through and had forgotten their role.

So, after almost a year of living with my parents, of feeling like they were trying to control my life, and dealing with their constant fighting, I was truly ready to move out. Ready to take on the challenge of being a single, working mother and going to school full-time. It was about my daughter's health and safety, our future. So, I moved into my mom's rental temporarily, but the two weeks I lived there were a total nightmare.

The house wasn't finished being renovated and was still under construction. There were no beds, the shower was dirty, there was no furniture and there was dust and dirt everywhere. That first night I tried to settle in as best as I could, using a cot and small pillows and a blanket as a bed for Sophia and I, but I couldn't sleep and Sophia wasn't happy. I fed her, soothed her and tried to get her to sleep, but she wouldn't stop crying. I lost my patience and had to go in another room to calm myself down. This was a real low point in my life. When I had saved up enough money I moved into my own apartment, where I lived for about six months before moving back into my mom's rental across the street (which by then was finished being renovated) so I could save money.

After I moved out, it seemed to me like no one in my family offered me any help. They didn't call me, didn't offer support, or to watch Sophia anymore. I think they didn't want to be involved in the drama between my mom and me. I felt totally abandoned, first by Derek, and now by my parents and the rest of my family.

After almost a year of grieving for Derek and not being able to talk to anyone about how much I missed him, of fighting with my parents and losing the little support from my family that I had, of no one really wanting to talk but to blame everything on me, and of being left with no one to help me get through school or help watch Sophia, I started to get bitter and hate the situation I found myself in.

I started feeling hate for Derek; for the choices he had made and for leaving me alone, to carry all this stress on my shoulders. I also felt so damn bad for Sophia. She was such a perfect daughter. She deserved it all, but instead she was dealt a childhood with no father and a mother struggling to get on her feet. I started feeling like I was failing at being a parent, which is the worst feeling in the world.

Once the newspaper article about my mom's arrest that ran in our local paper got picked up by the national media, everything became that much more stressful. By now, the first season of *Teen Mom* had already aired and our fan base was growing more and more. Having our private family issues made so public caused an even bigger rift between me and my family. They resented being bothered by reporters and nosey neighbors wanting information about me and the family—and who can blame them?

People around me began acting like they knew all about me, that my private issues were their business. I had cut myself off from my old life and now only had party buddies, so when the shit hit the fan I had no one to call, no one to really be a friend. At school, the one place where I had been able to escape from it all, my teachers were constantly asking me if I was okay. Of course, I said I was. But my projects started reflecting a lack of focus, because I really wasn't okay.

The worst part of this period of my life was having to leave Sophia with childcare providers that I didn't know. Because my mother was no longer allowed to babysit Sophia and money was so tight, the only childcare I could afford were babysitters from a list provided to me by the DHS.

At one point I went through five different state babysitters in two months. I hated leaving her, but by this point I only had three weeks of classes left until the end of the quarter and I desperately needed help with Sophia so I could work and get to class.

Finally, I told my parents about the situation. At the end of the day, despite all our issues, they loved Sophia unconditionally and agreed to watch her as often as they could, even if this meant they both had to watch her together until it was okay for my mom to be alone with Sophia again. I was relieved.

Hey Sophia!! your mom wanted to write you a letter, because We've now known Each other for a year now 😊 + I wanted to say I'm so happy I'm with you after going through Everything that I have I would say i'm thinking in the sence of (the past 2 years) so a little before I was pregnant with you till now a year later. I love you so much + I'm working so hard for us. But also I wanted to tell you that literally Everyone in the world thinks your the most gorgeous baby girl Ever! + your more popular then ~~other~~ other celebrity baby's! + Just to let you know you were born a star. So many people wished you a happy 1st birthday, Probably over 1,000 so that is a achievement!!, But I thought i'd say we've started out with no car + living with grandma to now moved out in our own wonderful place + a car + I'm working hard to graduate this year 2010 or by the beginning of 2011 from college So we can move away from Iowa + soon open our restraunt. I'm so excited; + I also hope you love your baby book + remember even if your dad can't be with us, he always cares and wishes us the best, I miss him so much sophia, I can't even express →

but I'm strong because of you! but
I hope maybe one day I'll find a guy
who you & I like who can be part of
our lives & impact in positivly & who
you & I can be friends with. that
would make me happy but it's not
needed & no one will ever replace your
dad. Your dad was my first love &
it's so hard to try to move on 🙁 right
now I don't think I'll ever fall in love
with a guy ever again * but I can
give you information & support when
you think you've maybe found a guy,
but I hope you will wait till your 21 !
I love you Sophia & I Just want
you to trust me to help you,
that's why I'm your Mom & God
made us for each other so your
all i need. xoxo I'll write you more
but it's bedtime! (right now your
            sleeping)
        & I love kissing
        your cheeky's &
        cuddling ☺

AFTER 1 YEAR

# STORMY WEATHER

A couple of months later, just as my life was starting to settle down, I got served with papers from Derek's mom. She was suing me for visitation rights to Sophia. But, as I argued in the court papers, she had never seen Sophia, never offered to pay for anything for her, never even sent her a birthday card or a gift.

I had been trying to get benefits for Sophia from Social Security, so I had reached out to Derek's sister. I needed someone from his family to supply a DNA sample to compare with Sophia's. If it was a match then I would be able to prove that Derek was Sophia's dad and she would be entitled to Social Security benefits. I hoped that since she was a new mom, too, that his sister would relate to where I was coming from and help me get Sophia's benefits.

At first, I was worried it would be hard to get her to commit to helping me. But once my lawyer contacted her she agreed to meet with me and provide the sample.

A few days later we got together at a park near the testing center, so she could meet Sophia and then come with me to do the DNA testing. The MTV crew was there to film it for season two of *Teen Mom*. It was very emotional seeing her. This was the first time since Derek's death that I had seen anyone from his family. She brought her daughter and an album with photos of Derek for Sophia.

She told me that she had talked to Derek before he died and that he had told her that he had planned to be there for me after the baby was born, no matter what. That I was his first and only love and that, even if the baby wasn't his, he was going to be there for me. I felt so sad hearing that. My one big regret is that I never got to hear him say those things to me himself before he died.

As much as I wanted to have a relationship with Derek's sister, for Sophia's sake, eventually it got too awkward because she was always trying to talk me into letting her mom be around if we were going to meet up. I gave her my number to give to her mother and I said that if her mom wanted to see Sophia she could call and talk to me about it directly.

After that, Derek's mom and I texted back and forth a couple of times, trying to arrange a time for her to meet with me and Sophia, but every time I suggested a meeting she had some reason that she couldn't make it. I was worried that she was just playing games and decided to send her a text letting her know that I didn't want her in my life or my daughter's life.

I thought that would be the end of it, so I was taken completely by surprise when I got served with papers from her, suing me for visitation rights to Sophia. I had a hard time believing she genuinely wanted to be a part of Sophia's life.

I decided that I didn't want her seeing Sophia. I wanted to fight her lawsuit. So I got a lawyer, and a court date was set. On the appointed day, I went to the courthouse and waited in the hall with my mom for the outcome of the hearing. My lawyer told me that, in order to win the case, Derek's mom would have to prove that I was an unfit mother and that she already had a relationship with my daughter. If she could prove those things, then she would have the right to force me to let her see Sophia. I didn't see how she could prove it, though. She had never had a relationship with my daughter.

Still, at the courthouse, I was nervous. After waiting for thirty anxious minutes, my lawyer came out of the courtroom and told us that I had won. I was so relieved to be able to put the whole thing behind me. Then I had my lawyer take all the information from this court case and send it to the Social Security office. With that evidence, and the DNA test from Derek's sister, which proved with 99.65% accuracy that he was the father, I was able to ultimately get survivor benefits for Sophia.

I just wanted Sophia to be able to get her benefits. The whole thing had been dragging on for almost a year by this point and I just wanted to get it over with so I never had to deal with Derek's mom ever again.

# MOVING FORWARD

Meanwhile, I still had to finish my last quarter of school and I was more stressed out than ever. I was torn between wanting to work hard and feeling like I just wanted to get it over with so I could spend more time with Sophia. I felt like I was constantly playing catch-up in both areas of my life.

I had always thought that I would have my college degree before I had a baby. Things hadn't worked out that way, but I still desperately wanted to get my degree so that I could keep moving forward *with* Sophia. I was terrified of being left behind or finding myself stuck where I was for the rest of my life.

Even though my goal was now within reach, this was a real low point in my life. I felt suicidal when I thought about how my life had turned out. Nothing had worked out like I had dreamed it would in those early days with Derek. Instead of us going off to college together, moving into our own place, getting married and living happily ever after, Derek was gone and I was raising our child on my own— and I was only nineteen!

On top of that I had been fighting with my parents at home and with

Derek's mom in court. All I wanted was to be able to give Sophia a happy childhood, but up until now it had been filled with legal battles and arrests. I felt like we would never be able to live normal lives.

Those last couple of weeks of college were hard. I was overwhelmed from the stress of the court case with Derek's mom, dealing with Derek death, and not being able to spend as much time with Sophia as I wanted. Sometimes I would just break down and start crying in the middle of class. I would have to take time-outs during the day. I was an emotional wreck.

I actually messed up so badly on my A La Carte Cooking final that I had to retake it. I was supposed to make the meal, set it up, and fire it out to the table, but my biscuits were horrible and my meat was overdone. I felt like my mind was so clogged up by stress that I couldn't remember how to do the simplest things. Two days later, as I was driving to school to retake the final, a song came on the radio that Derek and I used to listen to, back when we were happy, before all the fighting and lying started. It made me remember how good life seemed back then. Instead of feeling sad, it got me thinking about how good life could be again. It helped me pull myself together and focus enough to get through the final.

At this point, it became clear to me that I needed help processing everything I was going through. I realized for the first time that I had never properly grieved Derek's death. I had been bottling up my emotions because I needed to be strong for Sophia. Now it was time to really deal with my feelings about losing Derek and how my life had turned out.

Being thrust into adulthood—not to mention the public eye—so abruptly had been traumatic. I barely recognized my life anymore. One minute I was a sixteen-year-old cheerleader in a rocky relationship, the next I was a single mother and reality-TV star.

I started going to counseling. It was good for me to be able to talk to someone impartial who could guide me through difficult situations and set me straight when I was wrong. Having this outlet helped me process all the traumatic changes in my life—getting pregnant, losing Derek, and becoming a teen mom. It helped me deal with the bad feelings that came from my insecurities and struggles with motherhood.

I still go to counseling to help me stay on track and process my grief. I want to stay positive and not be sad around Sophia. I want to truly enjoy what the world has to offer. It's an ongoing process and I'm not ashamed to admit that I need help dealing with being a single mom.

In the end I worked through my finals, passed, and graduated with my Associate's Degree. I was both happy and relieved to be able to end that chapter of my life. I felt like now I could move forward and continue my education, but at a regular speed so that I could really enjoy it, and enjoy my child as well.


After I graduated, I started thinking back to what it was I had wanted to do before I got pregnant. I had always wanted to go away for college, and I realized that this was something I could still do. I had always dreamed about being in my twenties, living on my own and not having to answer to anyone, but going to college also meant so much more than that—it was about freedom and being part of something bigger than what I had known in my hometown.

I remembered a time when I was a sophomore in high school and a representative from the Minneapolis Art Institute came to give a talk in my computer class. I remembered the feeling I had when she spoke about going off to college. I found myself taking what she had to say much more seriously than I had expected. There was a whole world out there and I was hungry to be part of it.

So I did some research into places where I could get a bachelor's degree in Culinary Management. I considered a bunch of different schools in different states, but in the end my first choice was the Art Institute of Fort Lauderdale in Florida. I wanted a warm place. I was tired of the cold. Sophia and I needed sunshine and warmth in our lives, for a change.

# THE SUNSHINE STATE

When I got the news that I had been accepted to the Art Institute of Fort Lauderdale, I was elated. Finally, Sophia and I would have the chance to spread our wings and begin a new life together. We could leave behind the stress of teen motherhood, losing Derek, and battling with his family and mine. This would be our new beginning.

The only hitch was that I still had to break the news to my parents. I wasn't sure how they would feel about Sophia and I moving so far away.

Surprisingly, when I first told them about my plans, they were happy for me, but then it sunk in that I was moving soon and I was taking Sophia with me. After that, it became a struggle with them.

They worried about me moving so far away with Sophia and argued that it would be too stressful being on my own, with no one to help watch Sophia. They reminded me of all the issues I had had in the past with baby-sitters. My mom wanted me to leave Sophia with her, while I went to school. I resented that it felt like she was challenging my ability to make the right choice with Sophia and it became a source of tension in the lead up to my move.

As much as I tried to understand how hard it was going to be on her to be so far away from Sophia, I needed her to understand that *I* was the parent and the best place for Sophia to be was with *me*. I had them come with me to counseling so we could work through our issues and, in the end, we were able to work through the conflict without a lot of drama.

Of course, it bothered me that my parents didn't seem to think I could handle the situation, but instead of letting it consume me I decided to use it as motivation to prove to them, and everyone else, that I could handle being on my own. I'd made mistakes in the past, but I had learned from them. I was strong enough now to take care of myself and my daughter.

Because of all resentment I was having towards my parents, at first, I couldn't feel much sadness about moving. I just wanted to put every bad thing that had happened to me over the past couple of years behind me. I was ready to move forward and be on my own with Sophia. But as the day for me to leave got closer, I let my guard down and started to feel sad.

I realized that my parents had gone through a lot over the past couple of years, just like I had, and when they complained or gave me a hard time it was their way of dealing with it all. I knew they really loved me and Sophia so I was sad that they wouldn't be right across the street from us anymore and wouldn't be there to watch Sophia when I went to school anymore. We agreed that, no matter what, if I felt overwhelmed when we moved, Sophia could stay with them while I got settled.

# MOVING DAY

My dad helped me pack up all my things from my mom's house, while my mom watched Sophia. With a lot of heavy lifting and long sweaty hours, we moved everything out in one day.

I was really grateful for their all their help. Yes, it's still hard for me being around my parents at times, but our relationship is improving from when I was a teenager who had no clue what the world really was like, and they were an unhappily married couple who allowed stress to get the better of them. Now, instead of fighting and lashing out at each other, we are learning that when we disagree we can have a real conversation and work through our problems as adults.

Moving to Florida was crazy time, and I was glad my parents were there for me. I had to fly to Los Angeles to do a Public Service Announcement with the other Teen Moms as part of our work with MTV to help prevent teen pregnancy, so Sophia stayed with my mom for a week and my dad got stuck driving my car and a trailer full of my stuff to Florida all by himself. He made it all the way from Iowa to Florida in two days. By the time we met up in Ft.

Lauderdale, I was exhausted from working and taking the red eye and my dad was half-deranged from driving for forty-eight hours straight.

But, there was no rest for the weary. At the place I was moving into, they only allowed you to unpack during certain hours, so with both of us half-starved and sleep-deprived, we got our butts moving. For five straight hours we trudged through the rain, hauling all my stuff up in an elevator and down a long hallway to my new apartment.

I did lose my mind a little. I yelled at my dad and my dad yelled at me (being filmed during this process definitely added a little tension to the whole thing), but we are family and sometimes families yell. It was a tremendous bonding experience for us and it changed our relationship for the better.

After my dad and I showered, ate, and slept, our senses started coming back to us. We were able to look back at the previous day and laugh at how mean we were to each other and say, "Wow we accomplished so much," and I was able to thank him for all of his help.

My dad stayed at my place while I went back to Iowa to collect Sophia and bring her back to Florida to our new home. It was such a happy and proud moment for me. After couple of months, my dad left and I finally I had my first real taste of what it was like to truly be on my own. It was such an amazing bonding experience for me and Sophia.

My last two weeks of my first quarter at my new school in Florida were very challenging and, to be honest, I was definitely a little overwhelmed. I was trying to date and make friends in this new place, and trying to find reliable childcare. Everything was kind of too much up in the air and I didn't want to flunk my classes. I had also decided that after this quarter I wanted to switch schools.

I was excited about all of the changes, but Sophia and I needed a break. So, as much as I hated to be apart from her, my mom and I decided that Sophia should stay with her for a little while until I figured all of this out.

One important thing realized during this time on my own was that I am ready for more than what the average twenty-something guy has to offer. Maybe this has something to do with how fast I have evolved as a person. The things that are important to me are my education, my career, my family, and creating a safe environment in which Sophia can grow and learn. I realized I had been putting myself out in the dating world just to get hurt and waste time.

This was a big wake up call for me and it hit home hard when I found myself alone, truly alone, while Sophia was with my mom. So after a month, I called my mom to tell her I was coming to get Sophia. I had missed her so much, I cried when I saw her. I know now that the right place for her is with me; no one can give her the love and support that I can.

She knows I love her no matter what—no matter if she spills food all over the couch, poops on the floor, throws baby powder all over her room, and never wants to sleep in her own bed, she knows I will love her through all the tough times.

# UNHAPPY HOLIDAYS

My first Christmas in Florida was amazing, but it had been years since I had been able to enjoy the holidays. Ever since I got pregnant, Christmas had been really a hard time for me. Three years ago, I was pregnant and by myself, wishing Derek was with me to receive the first of our baby gifts. Wishing he would change, fearing that he wouldn't. Three days later, he died and that left me crying privately for a year.

The following Christmas, I was angry. To cope, I started going out and drinking and dating. It helped me pass the time and kept me numb. I showed up for Christmas and played Santa with Sophia, but I was still grieving and was only going through the motions for her sake.

The next year, I was completely paranoid—crazy brain. I wasn't myself at all. I quit wearing makeup and doing my hair. I stayed in my house for three days straight that Christmas. All I could think about was killing myself, and I was paralyzed by this fear that someone was going to break into my house. I felt like I was a horrible mom to Sophia and I was crying all the time because I missed Derek so much. It felt like it could only get worse. We did gifts at my parents' house that Christmas, but for the most part I kept to myself because I didn't want anyone seeing me as sad as I was.

The Christmas after I moved to Florida, for the first time, I was happy to go back home for the holidays, happy to be alive, and happy to be in the holiday spirit. The stress of school had lifted and moving away helped free me from the past. I was able to pursue some of the things that I had always wanted to do, and, best of all, I had so much more time to spend with Sophia. That was the Christmas I started singing again. I began enjoying everything that was in front of me…happy to finally be myself again.

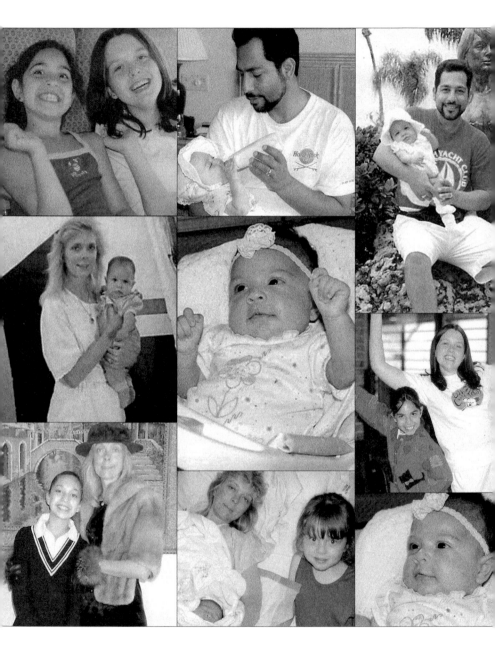

# FINALLY GETTING UP
# FROM ROCK BOTTOM

Since I've been in Florida I've made it a priority to be in contact with my parents and to stay on the best possible terms with them. We have been through so much together and they have made a real effort to change the things that drive me crazy, but mostly I have finally learned to accept them for who they are.

Growing up, my favorite memories are of when my mom and I would sit on the front porch at night and look at all the stars. I loved that. Summers where we lived were the best, we would be outside all day in the sun, gardening, biking, going on walks. I loved running as a kid, so every day I would go running at the track by my house. When I think back to all these times, I feel sad that it went by so quickly.

But what I also remember about my childhood was always having to go to my grandparents' house, because my parents were constantly working and traveling. I loved my grandparents' house, my grandma would be being canning and you could smell the tomatoes and peppers all day, but it wasn't my home. I just wanted my parents to be around more.

I have a vivid memory from when I was three or four years old, I was outside in our backyard, crying as I was walking away from my parents around to the back door of our house. I don't remember why I was crying, but I remember that I always felt like I wasn't loved enough. They were always working, or out of town, or fighting. I remember always having to be patient, to wait my turn for their attention, but it seemed like it was never my turn.

I made a promise to myself back then, *One day I will move away, I will be on my own and I won't need anybody.* So, growing up, that's why I never really hung onto friends, because I felt like I'd be gone soon anyway. I didn't want to care about anyone or have attachments that would hold me back. I just felt like there must be something more for me out there in the world.

When I met Derek, he was the one person whom I got caught up in and for whom I broke all my rules. I let my guard down because he made me feel loved in the way I needed. When I first met Derek, we shared the same dream. We talked about moving away and having our own place. I believed he would take care of me, love me for who I was, and be there for me when I needed him. Even when everything started going wrong with our relationship, it was hard for me to walk away because I couldn't let go of the dream.

Now I realize that was why it was so hard for me to deal with getting pregnant. By that time, Derek had shown that he wasn't ready to break away from his self-destructive habits or the toxic things in his life that were bringing him down. He acted like the love between us was nothing, talked badly about me and my family, and I had caught him in lie after lie.

The truth of how he had changed finally began to sink in on the day I called him to tell him I was pregnant and he didn't pick up. Instead I went home and had to tell my mom. In the end, it was my family that was there to support me—not Derek. I still held on to my dream though, hoping that after I had the baby Derek would grow into the man I needed him to be.

When he died, that dream died with him.

The day Sophia was born was both the happiest and saddest of my life. She was so precious and beautiful, but I couldn't look at her without seeing Derek. Her toes were his toes, the shape of her face, her ears, her hands—all Derek. When I got out of the hospital I realized that I had to stay home and finish college. I couldn't move away yet. I was forced to let go of my teenage dream once and for all and I felt like I had let myself down. The grief began to catch up with me and I sank into depression.

When I finally began to pull myself out of depression, I realized how much I was setting myself back and letting myself down as a parent. There was still so much to live for, I just needed to find my independent self again.

I did get to move away, after all. I'm on my own now, making my own rules and learning the limitations of what I can handle on my own. Sometimes I feel like I'm in a race against time. There's so much I want to do. I feel it at night, like a giant clock ticking inside my head. I can't get to sleep sometimes because I feel like I have so much I want to do in life and I have no more time to make bad choices and get off track.

# A NEW DREAM

I still miss Derek. I always will. This past year, on the third anniversary of his car accident, I sat down with Sophia and showed her pictures of her father. I pulled out a black photo album with our prom picture on the cover and sat down next to her on her bed.

I held the book open and began showing her all the photos I had been able to collect of Derek. It felt great to have this moment with her and I realized I had been waiting for this day from the moment she was born.

There is so much to tell her about her father and this is the only way she will ever get to know him. I showed her school photos from his freshmen year to his senior year, and talked about how he changed during those years. I showed her his childhood photos and I told her how much she looked like her daddy, how cute he was and how pretty she is. I told her why I loved her dad and how much I loved him.

As we looked through the photos, memories of our life together flashed through my mind; of our first prom and the night I lost my virginity to him, of the night I escaped from what would have been his senior prom and we went out dancing all night; how he would hold me against him as we stared at each other in his bedroom mirror.

I started this photo album after I received photos from Derek's sister the day we met at the park, because I finally had enough pictures to fill a small album. I wish I had more photos to show Sophia, but I have to be content with the ones I have and with the memories of her father that I have to share with her.

It makes me so sad that Derek and Sophia never had a chance to meet, but I try to keep it positive and just share as much about him as I can with her. Now that she can talk, she tells me "I'm proud of you mommy" and "I love you mommy." It makes me want to work harder. She helps me see that even though nothing worked out the way I had wanted it to, her happiness is what is most important.

I am finally able to put my past where it belongs—behind me. I've come to terms with the choices I've made. Of course, I have regrets. If I had known how things would turn out, there is so much I would have done differently. First and foremost, I would never have cut off communication with Derek two months before his car accident. I would have marched right up to him and told him straight to his face that I was pregnant with his child.

Sometimes, when I'm feeling alone and deserted, I wonder, *What if Derek was still here? Would we have grown apart or would we have grown up together?* I've learned so much from my experiences and I could have never have imagined I would be where I am today. I truly believe that I am doing the right thing by never settling for less than my teenage dream (even if that dream is now a little different from the one I had at sixteen).

For a while I thought that dream had died. I had so much on my plate (working, getting my degree, taking care of a newborn, repairing my relationship with my parents, and dealing with Derek's death) that I couldn't see that when Sophia was born the seed for a new dream had been planted.

I still dream of romance and happily ever after. I know that someday

I will find that one person with whom I will feel content, whose eyes I can stare into for hours, the way I used to do with Derek. But I have learned now that there is more to it than just that. I need someone who knows right from wrong, someone who knows how to cherish a relationship, someone who will be a positive male role model for my daughter, who understands my past and is happy to be part of my future. I haven't found that person yet, but the dream is what keeps me going.

As time has gone by and I have begun to heal, a new dream of making it in the world and being a role model for my daughter has taken shape. I guess we never stop dreaming. I've learned that although our dreams may die, if you open yourself up to life, new ones are born.